# Historic Homes of Florida

## Second Edition

*Laura Stewart and Susanne Hupp*

Pineapple Press, Inc.
Sarasota, Florida

# *Acknowledgments*

We are grateful to so many people for their contributions that it would be impossible to thank them all. But we particularly would like to express appreciation to the late Nancy Taylor, a Florida history buff, and Sherry Davich for their advice and helpful suggestions as we first undertook our research. For this newly revised and expanded edition, we also want to thank everyone at Pineapple Press for all of their work, especially intern Caitlyn Miller and assistant editor Helena Berg.

This book could not have been written without such sources as the park rangers of the Florida Department of Natural Resources and other agencies, who answered endless questions about their "charges"—the state's historic house museums. We are also grateful to the members of the many historical organizations who took the time to explain homes' complex histories and enthralling legends. Finally, and most of all, we dedicate this book to those who planned their homes for Florida's unique environment and building materials, those who built for the ages and not for the moment, and those who protect and restore the state's remarkable, fragile old houses, and thus its legacy.

Inquiries should be addressed to:
Pineapple Press, Inc.
P.O. Box 3899
Sarasota, Florida 34230

Library of Congress Cataloging in Publication Data

Stewart, Laura, 1947-
  Historic homes of Florida / Laura Stewart and Susanne Hupp.-- 2nd ed.
    p. cm.
  "Newly revised and expanded edition"--Acknowledgments.
  Includes index.
  ISBN-13: 978-1-56164-417-9 (pbk. : alk. paper)
  1. Dwellings--Florida--Guidebooks. 2. Bed and breakfast accommodations--Florida--Guidebooks. 3. Restaurants--Florida--Guidebooks. 4. Florida--Guidebooks. I. Hupp, Susanne, 1927- II. Title.
  F312.H87 2008
  917.5904'64--dc22
                        2008008896

Second Edition
10 9 8 7 6 5 4 3 2 1

Design by Shé Heaton
Printed in China

# Contents

# *Preface*

Better than history books and lectures, houses tell the stories of a place's past. They are where the pioneers and politicians, the merchants and millionaires, the teachers and homemakers, the writers and gardeners and families lived their private lives; they are the most personal architecture. Looking at houses—examining their sizes and materials and amount of ornamentation or its lack—is a lively way to trace a region's growth and links to the larger world, as well as local lore.

Houses—at least the handful of houses that survive the passage of time, shifting styles, and problems of progress—show the changes their many owners made to them as years went by and fortunes, too often, faded. Houses, in short, show the human side of history. Those in *Historic Homes of Florida* were built in simpler, quieter times. Most stood on large lots in small towns, and were the proudest expressions of their owners' tastes and ambitions. Like the happy dwelling in *The Little House* by Virginia Lee Burton, most of the houses in this book have seen their share of ups and downs and, almost miraculously, they still stand today as proud testaments to our state's heritage and to the devotion of the people who, literally, loved them.

All of the homes in this book are at least fifty years old and are open to the public, most as house museums. The others are restaurants or bed-and-breakfast inns. They offer a cross-section of the sorts of homes Floridians made for themselves during the past two hundred years or so. Not all are the homes of wealthy people. Many are simple structures built by pioneers who struggled in the often difficult climate of the region, before and after it became a state. All, however, open doors onto the history of a place that has seen some of the bloodiest wars and the strangest activities, from houses that sheltered shipwreck survivors to homes built with salvage from shipwrecks.

Better than anything else, Florida's old houses tell Florida's fascinating story.

# Introduction

# The Heritage of Florida

Gamble Plantation, Ellenton

I
The Panhandle

II
Northeast
Florida

III
Central
Florida

IV
Southwest Florida

V
South
Florida

VI
The Keys

# Land of Opportunity

Tall, glittering buildings dot Florida's rapidly growing city skylines, and eager visitors flock to its beaches and tourist attractions. Every day, an estimated eight hundred people move to Florida, drawn by its sunshine and warmth, its groves and glades, and its promise and potential.

But nearly invisible behind that booming reality stands another—an older and equally intriguing—Florida. It is a region that is surprisingly rich in history and legends. Many of its buildings stand as vivid testimony to its conglomeration of settlers. The architectural evidence stretches back well into prehistoric times—nearly four thousand years before Juan Ponce de León claimed Florida for Spain, naming it Pascua Florida (feast of flowers) on April 2, 1513, for the religious holiday of Easter.

Long before it became the vacation spot for students on spring break and families seeking tourist attractions, before Henry Plant and Henry Flagler built railroads through the state, before high society wintered in Palm Beach, before wreckers salvaged goods from ships in the Keys, before settlers and natives clashed in the Seminole Wars, and even before Confederate leaders sought refuge as the South fell, Florida was the land of golden opportunity to a variety of newcomers, from conquistador to developer, who have left a mark on Florida's architectural heritage.

The earliest known manmade monuments in Florida, the mysterious shell circles found along the St. Johns River, were built by a long-vanished race known simply as the Ancient People. They, like the Native Americans who inhabited Florida as the centuries passed, probably lived in huts made of available material such as wood and palm thatch. Spanish settlers later adopted this form of housing.

If early reports may be believed, however, the early dwellers built more than simple huts, shell circles, and mounds. The Spaniard Hernando de Soto, who landed near Tampa Bay in 1539, painted a glowing picture of Florida's rich resources and architectural heritage. Immense, fantastic temples were decorated with shells, pearls, and mica sand that caught the light and dazzled the eyes, according to one legend. Fabulous jewels and brightly dyed, painted, and beaded garments were to be seen everywhere.

The earliest European dwellings were less glamorous, although their builders also made use of Florida's abundant natural materials. To defend their holdings from English explorers plying the coasts and French Huguenots seeking safe haven from religious intolerance, the Spanish in 1565 established St. Augustine, the nation's first permanent European settlement.

It would be another century before construction began on the thick-walled Castillo de San Marcos, the oldest masonry building in America, but already a city was growing around the earlier wooden strongholds that had protected Florida's economic center. St. Augustine's earliest residents lived in "straw shelters," described by Franciscan monks as "wretched huts that scarce protect us from weather." In the early days, houses made of wood or daub-and-wattle and palm thatch were common. Then, as the massive walls of the Castillo took shape, formed of coquina—a soft, pale, local limestone containing broken coral and seashells—homes, too, began to be constructed of the material.

The stone was held together by tabby, a primitive form of concrete made by mixing lime, crushed shells, sand, and water. Such early St. Augustine structures as the Oldest House, built before 1715, and the Peña Peck House have solid coquina bases that provide protection from heat and hurricanes. Residences typically had balconies and wooden second stories made of hewn cedar. Roofs were thatched.

By 1763, when thriving St. Augustine's population had surpassed three thousand, Spain ceded Florida to England and most Spanish residents left the region. For nearly twenty years, Britain ruled a vast colony divided into eastern and western regions. St. Augustine was the capital of East Florida. Pensacola was the capital of West Florida, which was bounded by the Mississippi River to the west, the Apalachicola and Chattahoochee Rivers to the east, and approximately the thirty-first parallel to the north.

British rule lasted only twenty years, but it left an indelible imprint on Florida, modifying the dominant Spanish style of architecture and creating the well-ordered social systems and plantation economy that proved crucial for the state's growth. It was a period during which Florida changed considerably and its population became far more varied.

Debtors and beggars were recruited from Britain to help establish Rollestown, long since vanished, before moving to St. Augustine. Greek, Italian, and Minorcan immigrants settled in New Smyrna. By the 1770s, when the Revolutionary War raged and England used a sympathetic Florida as a base of operations, one hundred plantations in East Florida were producing crops that were very valuable to England: indigo, sugar, turpentine, citrus, tobacco, and rice. For the most part, Floridians were British sympathizers who chose not to

The architectural influence of Spanish rule shows in the Ximeniz-Fatio house.

side with the thirteen colonies.

As that struggle drew to a close and British defeat seemed certain, Florida's first land boom began. About twelve thousand loyalists fled Georgia and the Carolinas, bringing their architectural traditions to Florida. Typical changes may be seen in St. Augustine, where homes were altered and expanded to suit their new owners' tastes, as well as to make them more comfortable during warm and damp seasons.

Flammable, perishable thatched roofs were replaced with durable wooden shakes and, to provide relief from heat and rain, early "Florida rooms"—called loggias—were added to many structures. Balconies, arches, and stucco-style finishes remained, however, and the Spanish flavor was fixed in Florida.

In 1783, with Spain once again in control, another exodus of Florida residents began— this time of British loyalists to England, nearby colonies, and the wilderness of the American West. But the English-inspired place names, boundaries, political systems, religious diversity, plantation economy, and design development did not leave with their creators.

The captain's office and a ship's hatch on the roof reflect the influence of one of the early owners of Key West's oldest house.

Little by little, Spain permitted settlement of Florida by runaway slaves and citizens of the new United States. As the settlers became more restless and demanding under foreign rule, the region became difficult to hold. Fertile, prosperous Florida was an enticing region for the aggressive young nation. After an overwhelming number of problems in the faraway colony, including land seizures and bloody incursions by the United States, Spain agreed to sell Florida. In 1819, Spain signed its unruly colony over to the States for $5 million—which Spain never received. And two years later, after almost three hundred years of Spanish rule, Florida became a U.S. territory.

It would be another twenty-four years before Florida became a state, but those short decades saw tremendous changes in the territory. Hot-tempered Andrew Jackson, who had led two violent and illegal raids into Florida during Spanish domination, ruled briefly as governor, and the division into eastern and western sections was eliminated. A new city midway between the former capitals of East and West Florida, Tallahassee, became the capital in 1823.

Despite the suffering brought about by the seven-year Seminole Wars—fought as the remnant of a number of native tribes struggled to avoid deportation—the unified Florida flourished. Even before it attained statehood in 1845 with a population of fifty-seven thousand, Florida had established an agrarian economy, and peace and prosperity allowed the construction of a number of gracious antebellum manor houses.

The land appealed to settlers as varied as Maj. Robert Gamble, who had established his sugarcane plantation in Ellenton, near

Bradenton, after fighting in the bloody Seminole Wars, and Prince Achille Murat, nephew of Napoleon Bonaparte and a planter drawn to Florida's promising future.

Gamble's mansion is typical of the period's style, with stately columns, broad verandas, and use of indigenous materials—here, the familiar tabby—but it is the only one outside the Florida Panhandle still standing. Bellevue, the simple frame home the prince built to replace his log cabin in Tallahassee, is less distinguished architecturally than Gamble's mansion, but it shows the practical vernacular approach many took when building homes on new plantations.

Most were as unpretentious, though very likely as comfortable, as Live Oak Plantation, a two-storied frame structure built with wide, ground-level porches by Gov. John Branch before 1840. Like many of Florida's older historic homes, the Leon County residence no longer exists. It survived until 1894, when it was destroyed by fire, but many less ostentatious homes were dismantled around 1850, to be replaced by much grander versions.

Interestingly, one landowner who never developed his Tallahassee property was the famous French hero of the American Revolution, Gen. Marquis de Lafayette. Accused first of keeping his land off the market to increase its value, then of trying to sell it in lots for a greater profit, the impoverished aristocrat finally sold it piecemeal before dying in 1834. His dream had been to grow vines, olives, and mulberry tress on the land, which would be worked by French peasants. He wanted to create a model community and help end slavery.

While an agricultural economy was evolving in central and northern Florida, the southern end of the state remained relatively undeveloped, except for Key West. Isolated from the mainland, the two-by-four-mile island had become the most populous city in Florida by 1850. Its economy was far simpler than that in northern Florida. Located on the hazardous but well-traveled Florida Straits, Key West became, in the eighteenth century, home to West Indian fishermen (traditionally called Conchs because of their fondness for the shellfish) and later to other residents and wreckers who salvaged goods from ships that came to grief on the Florida Reef. Although piracy was suppressed by the U.S. government after Florida became a territory in 1821, wrecking was still big business in Key West when the Civil War began.

Key West's unique wooden houses reflect Bahamian, New England, Creole, and Victorian influences that together make up an indigenous architecture adapted to the tropics and inspired by ships' master carpenters. Early Conch houses were built in styles similar to those seen along the New England seacoast or in the Conchs' native Bahamas. Racy, raucous Key West was not typical of Florida, although the practicality of its architecture is typical of other indigenous residences that may still be seen throughout the state.

Built by small farmers and other new settlers, the so-called frame vernacular, or Cracker, house was made of split logs and raised off the ground for air circulation. Its roof of cypress shingles, steeply pitched, allowed hot air to rise high above the heads of people in the house, leaving the living space cool. During the early to mid-1800s, these log homes were almost identical in design. Typically, two similar rooms were built under a common roof and separated by a breezeway called a dogtrot. Both rooms served as combination bedrooms, dens, and sewing rooms. Wide front and back porches provided additional living areas and protected the house from the harsh summer sun. Meals were cooked in detached kitchens some twenty to thirty feet behind the main house. Kitchens were kept separate so that if fire started there, it would not spread to the rest of the house; the heat of the kitchens was also kept away from the home's living space.

Later in the century, more modern Cracker houses were built of board and batten using prefabricated balloon-frame technique, so that they could be raised in large pieces and quickly assembled. The houses were roofed with metal, had high ceilings, and also had inside shutters to close out the hot midday sun.

Until the Civil War, Florida's culture and economy revolved around the plantation, yet the state never had many large estates. Most of the plantations the state did have were in a huge arc curving from Jackson County through Marion County. About eighty plantations had more than a thousand acres each; fewer than fifty had more than one hundred slaves.

Contrary to myths about the elegant way of life led by leisured landowners, few had time to develop an elevated, enlightened lifestyle. Most were too busy working their land, and they led surprisingly precarious existences. The Kingsley Plantation on Fort George Island north of Jacksonville, now a

Thomas Edison and Henry Ford could relax and share their ideas on the porches of Mangoes, the Ford Winter Home in Ft. Myers.

national park, serves as an example of the less-than-glamorous life on a Florida plantation. Yet even the smallest cotton farmer aspired to the grandeur that was associated with life on a plantation.

The truth is that Florida in the mid-nineteenth century was still a rural, sparsely populated state. Before 1860, not one Florida town had more than three thousand inhabitants. Yet Florida was growing quickly. In 1845, the population was an estimated 66,500. Fifteen years later, it had increased by one hundred percent, and twelve new counties were carved out of earlier, general designations noted on maps.

When stirrings of the Civil War were felt in Florida, the state's economy and political alliances dictated its sympathies, which lay with the Confederacy. And with the coming of war, Florida found itself in a strategic position. Federal arsenals in Florida were seized by Confederate troops in 1861; soon after that, all but three U.S. forts were taken by the South.

Approximately fifteen thousand Floridians served in the Confederate Army, but the state's greatest contributions to the war effort were material—Florida provided beef and other food to the blockaded South—and geographic. Its shoreline offered refuge to Confederate ships, while the Union's forts in the Keys and at Santa Rosa Island, near Pensacola, allowed warships to sail in search of Confederate blockade runners. The state's tremendous productivity during the war brought it to the attention of the North, and Union forces fought to conquer the interior during the final years. On March 6, 1865, a band of children, old men, and a few soldiers held off Union forces at Natural Bridge near Tallahassee, saving the capital

from capture by Union forces. In the end, of course, the South fell, though Tallahassee was the only Confederated Capital east of the Mississippi River not to be captured during the war; on May 20, 1865, Federal forces entered Tallahassee unopposed.

Unlike its impoverished Southern neighbors, the state entered a prosperous era. Gone were the days of slavery and plantations; soon after the end of the War Between the States, Florida became a paradise for sportsmen, for tourists, and particularly for consumptives and other invalids. A decade after the war ended, the great Southern poet Sidney Lanier traveled through Florida. In the guidebook he wrote, Lanier could barely contain his enthusiasm for the charms of the state.

Lanier—like other vacationers, settlers, and, increasingly, speculators—made his trip partly by trains jolting over track gauges, partly by wagon, and partly by steamboat. It surely was an entertaining journey. Some seasonal visitors to Florida, among them author Harriet Beecher Stowe, stayed in their own private homes in the state. The Stowes' was a lacily gabled, stick-style bungalow in Mandarin on the St. Johns River near Jacksonville. (It is no longer standing.)

As the century ended, though, seasonal visitors were able to winter in sprawling, elaborate hotels such as the triple-towered, frame Sanford or the grand Ponce de Leon in St. Augustine. The Ponce de Leon was one of the nations' first poured-concrete structures and the first to revive the Spanish style. By the late nineteenth century, Henry Flagler and Henry Plant had opened Florida to widespread tourism by laying smooth train tracks over most of the state and building spectacular hotels at each journey's end. In this eclectic era, any and every architectural style became the norm.

As tourism boomed, so did the state's population. Between 1860 and 1880, the population grew to almost 270,000 and included returning Union soldiers, visitors, and planters, many of whom came from far away to enjoy society or to raise citrus—or to speculate on land.

Paradise had its down side, however. A couple of cold days in the winter of 1894–95 changed Florida's history and gave rise to numerous legends. While guests enjoyed the amenities at Flagler's baronial Royal Poinciana Hotel in Palm Beach or Plant's Arabic/Moorish/Turkish Tampa Bay Hotel, the temperature outside dropped disastrously. Two successive freezes, one in December and the other in January, wiped out ninety percent of Florida's citrus crop. According to legend, a group of British planters who had settled in central Florida played polo while their trees froze, then packed up and returned to England. Those recent transplants were all second sons of wealthy Englishmen, who bought the land so that their sons would be suitably occupied. But, not understanding that such weather was unusual, the English growers abandoned groves that would again bear fruit. More importantly, they also left homes built in the ornate Victorian style that became part of the state's eclectic roster of historic buildings.

Another legend explains how Miami came about and a new section of Florida prospered. Just after the second freeze of 1894–95, Flagler was deeply concerned about the economy. Because of the freeze and the financial panic that had seized the country, his railroad had lost money. Surrounded by withered trees and

faced with loss of revenue, he opened a box of fresh green branches abloom with orange blossoms—sent to him from Miami by Julia Tuttle. She was determined to show Flagler that the weather was fine farther south. Encouraged, he employed men to push the railroad almost as far south as it could go.

At the same time, Plant was pushing through on the west coast. He built the six-hundred-room Hotel Belleview and its celebrated golf course in Clearwater. In addition, Florida's depressed economy was given a boost by the Spanish-American War of 1898, when troops were quartered in Tampa.

Residential architecture reflected the state's increased magnificence. "The Taj Mahal of America," Flagler's Whitehall in Palm Beach, opened in 1901. Like Newport, Lenox, and other posh Northeastern resorts built by *nouveau riche* industrial barons, Florida was home to palatial surroundings for the Gilded Age's leisure class. Opulent Whitehall was soon followed by James Deering's Villa Vizcaya in Miami, John Ringling's Cà d'Zan in Sarasota, and Addison Mizner's Spanish-style masterpieces in Palm Beach.

An influx of newcomers in the early 1900s brought the new colonial revival styles and an elegant classicism to northern and central Florida. In the 1920s, yet another boom brought a taste for the exotic and romantic. Just before the 1926 hurricane, which practically leveled Miami, developers such as George Merrick and Glenn Curtiss planned playful French, Italian, Chinese, and Arabian Nights communities at Coral Gables, Hialeah, and Opa-Locka in south Florida. Addison Mizner's 1920s Mediterranean designs in Palm Beach County, Miami's art deco houses and hotels of

Henry Flagler's railway brought growth that reshaped South Florida.

the 1930s, and James Gamble Rogers' fanciful central Florida homes added to an ever-richer and more complex roster of historic residences in the state.

The backdrop for all this architectural experimentation was one of fairly constant growth. In 1880, Florida had consisted of a few coastal cities, vast agricultural holdings, and the almost uninhabited—and, mostly, uninhabitable—south Florida. By 1920, the population had jumped from about a quarter of a million to a million. Six cities had more than ten thousand inhabitants; Jacksonville had almost a hundred thousand. The residents of Tampa numbered fifty thousand in 1920, while Miami was home to nearly thirty thousand. Once the coastal communities had been settled, people moved inland to the once-swampy Lake Okeechobee area.

By the turn of the twentieth century, a railroad route linked Jacksonville to Miami, running through central Florida and Palm Beach and encouraging settlement; on January 22, 1912, the first train pulled into Key West. The state's 54,005 farms were valued at more

than $330 million and produced an annual income of more than $80 million. After the devastating 1894–95 freezes, farmers and planters had diversified and citrus was grown farther south. Florida recovered from the 1926 hurricane, which hit from Miami across to the Gulf coast, as well as a hurricane that hit the eastern shores of Lake Okeechobee and the Palm Beach area in 1928. The hurricanes, coupled with the 1929 stock market crash, temporarily put an end to the state's fabled land boom. But the forgiving land continued to produce, and its fine weather attracted winter-weary people eager to escape to an Eden that included amusing architecture.

Even the state's educational institutions mirror its varied, eclectic nature. Near the end of the nineteenth century, Florida's first major universities, Florida State University in Tallahassee and the University of Florida in Gainesville, were founded, along with such sectarian colleges as Rollins in Winter Park and Stetson in DeLand. The varied styles of the schools—turreted Romanesque at FSU, lofty Gothic at the University of Florida, Victorian

Revival at Stetson, and Spanish Renaissance at Rollins—are as colorful as those of the state's hotels and homes. Florida's other buildings are just as diverse, reflecting the state's rich cultural and architectural heritage.

Far more forcefully, and personally, than the state buildings, college halls, and other public buildings, however, it is Florida's homes that tell the story of the state's history. Some residences, chief among them Flagler's in Palm Beach and Ringling's in Sarasota, are mansions with polished façades. But most of the homes in this guidebook were built to be lived in, as ever-evolving structures that reflected the successive lifestyles of their owners. Each residence included here is open to the public, most as house museums but a number as bed-and-breakfast inns or as restaurants.

All houses in *Historic Homes of Florida* were built at least fifty years ago, and all have interesting historic features. The book is divided into geographic districts so readers can select tours and plan trips, either in a small area for a brief day or weekend jaunt or to a distant region for an extended immersion into Florida's past. Even a day trip, however, might include meals in charming old homes that double as restaurants; overnight stays can enhance the effect of dipping into history if spent in a historic home. Maps and brief histories included in each of the book's sections place the homes geographically in the state, and historically in the bygone eras that created them.

# I

# The Panhandle

## The Panhandle

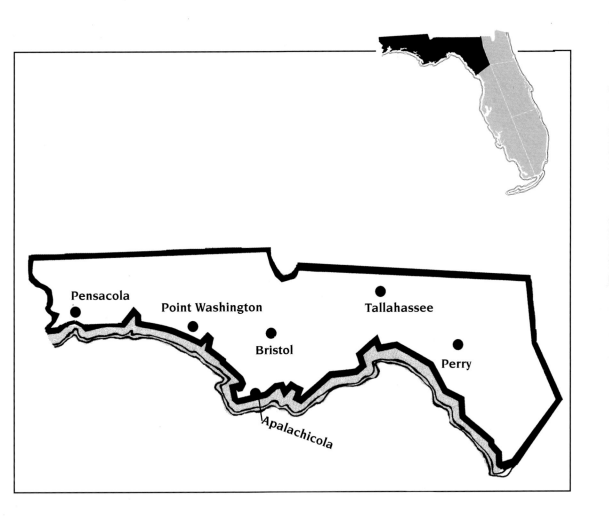

# The Old South

Early in the sixteenth century, when Spanish explorers first visited the hilly, timbered Panhandle, they found hostile Apalachee Indians already in residence. By the early 1630s, however, Spanish missionaries had established settlements in the region. The Panhandle remained part of the crown's North American holdings for more than a century, until Spain ceded Florida to England in 1763. During that first period of Spanish domination, it is believed that missionaries lived in wattle-and-daub structures with palm-thatch roofs—thus adapting native materials and techniques to new use.

While Tallahassee, Pensacola, and other Panhandle towns were under Spanish domination, they were small, Catholic communities. During the twenty years of British rule, from 1763 to 1783, the northern part of Florida was divided into the royal colonies of East and West Florida. It wasn't until the early 1800s that the region began to show significant development.

Rapid settlement began in the fertile, 2,300-square-mile area in the northwest soon after Florida became a territory of the young United States in 1821. In 1823, Tallahassee was chosen as the capital of the territory because of its location halfway between Pensacola and St. Augustine (the old capital cities of West and East Florida under the British). Tallahassee, which the Spanish missionaries had called San Luis, was given its name by Octavia Walton during territorial times. Daughter of a territorial governor and granddaughter of a signer of the Declaration

of Independence, she chose a word that means "old town" in the Creek Indian tongue.

By 1824, when three log cabins were constructed to house Florida's Legislative Council, Tallahassee had been designed on a grid pattern, with Capitol Square as the center. The first sale of lots was held in 1825. By the fall of that year, the town had fifty houses, seven stores, a church, a schoolhouse, an apothecary, and a printing shop around the new square—and was incorporated as a city. It also had the first of many ambitious homes, and more would follow. Tallahassee, with its nearby rich farming lands and potential for prosperity, attracted members of several wealthy Southern families. It also attracted the Marquis de Lafayette, a French hero of the Revolutionary War who never actually lived on his land, and Prince Achille Murat, a nephew of Napoleon Bonaparte who did settle in the state.

The city of Pensacola, far to the west in the Panhandle, was established in 1698 by the Spanish near the site of a colony that had been founded in 1559 by Tristan de Luna and abandoned two years later. It was in Pensacola that the transfer of the Floridas from Spain to the United States was arranged, and here that the capital of West Florida was established. By the mid-nineteenth century, the Panhandle was becoming a prime center for agriculture, particularly for cotton, as well as for the milling and shipping of lumber. Crackers—settlers from Mississippi, South Carolina, Virginia, and Georgia—arrived to build humble frame houses or cottages that adapted the styles of the Gulf coast and the inland South to the new climate. Wealthy planters from other states moved to the region, along with their slaves and a taste for the columned mansions and porch-wrapped plantations of the Gulf coast and South Carolina low country.

Florida's great Panhandle homes were raised from the ground to allow for maximum air circulation, as were most homes throughout the state. Verandas often stretched to two stories, providing shade from the subtropical sun and shelter from showers. And, like their counterparts elsewhere, Florida's plantations were built in such fashionable revivalistic styles as the Greek and bracketed Italianate.

The Civil War, however, destroyed the Southern way of life, and countless antebellum mansions fell into disrepair. After the war ended, many of the Panhandle's abandoned plantations were bought by Northerners for use as winter game preserves. The last two decades of the nineteenth century saw a shift from farming to hunting in Leon and Jefferson Counties, and tremendous tracts of land were held by new owners. In the Panhandle, as in the rest of Florida, the amazing mix of architectural styles that may be seen in old houses reflects the history of the region.

# Charles Lavalle House

*Pensacola*

The four-room Lavalle House was constructed between 1803 and 1815 by Charles Lavalle, a Pensacola builder. Lavalle, who probably came to Pensacola from Louisiana, also was part owner of a brickyard on Gull Point.

The small Creole cottage resembles others in Pensacola known to have been built during the last Spanish occupation, in as well as others built at that time along the Gulf coast. Its construction, however, was an unusual combination of brick and frame. The outer walls of the Lavalle House are made of beaded lap siding over brick, while interior walls were plaster over brick.

For the house's four-block move in 1968 to its present site in Historic Pensacola Village, bricks in three of the exterior walls and interior partitions were taken out and then reinstalled. One wall remained intact and is almost completely original, and even the original plaster remains on that wall. Floors are of random-width yellow pine.

Built on brick piers with a deeply recessed gallery porch under a gabled roof, the one-and-a-half-story house has four evenly spaced large doors on the front and back façades. Its steeply pitched roof is covered with cedar shingles, as it was when it was new. Two brick chimneys rise from the center of the roof.

The two front rooms adjoin each other; each opens into the identically sized room behind it, and fireplaces open into both rooms on each side of the house. One front room is now furnished as a bedroom, although it may have served as a main living room if, as is conjectured, two families occupied the house. A hidden stairway in one of the back rooms leads to an attic above that would have been used for sleeping and storage by the house's early owners. Although it is likely that the original house had a separate kitchen, one of the back rooms now fills that role.

The furnishings—some acquired in recent years from private donors and others purchased from antique dealers in Louisiana—are from the late eighteenth and early nineteenth century. A few of the pieces are of French origin, but the majority were probably made in rural Louisiana and elsewhere along the Gulf coast.

*The Lavalle House, 205 E. Church St. in Pensacola, is part of Historic Pensacola Village. Hours are 10 a.m. to 4 p.m. Monday through Saturday. Admission is charged. For further information, call (850) 595-5985.*

# Dorr House

*Pensacola*

This two-story, Greek Revival–style house in Pensacola was built for Clara Barkley Dorr. She was a young widow in 1849 when she married Eben Walker Dorr. Clara and their six children moved into the new yellow pine house in 1871, the year after Dorr died, and she lived there until 1895. Dorr was the son of Ebenezer Dorr, the last territorial marshal of West Florida and the first marshal of Escambia County when Florida became a state in 1845.

The house is considered significant because it is a well-preserved example of Greek Revival architecture. This style, popular in the rest of the country early in the century, persisted along the Gulf coast well after the Civil War, when home builders in the North had begun to adopt Gothic Revival and other high Victorian styles. Greek Revival decorative elements include dentil (or tooth-shaped) molding along the cornices of the building and the capitals of the columns. Like the Greek-style fret meander on the bay window's cornice, they reveal a fondness for the classical.

The house also is adapted to the climate: Its two-story porches shade the house and permit cooling breezes to flow through its high windows even on hot, rainy days. The home is raised above the ground on brick piers, and the lower part of the almost floor-to-ceiling windows on its façade may be opened like double doors to increase air circulation. Its interior kitchen was added well after the family moved in; the house probably originally had a separate kitchen, or it may have been designed without a kitchen. For two years after moving into the house, Clara Dorr paid board to her sister, who lived nearby.

When the house was new, the walls of its ground-floor rooms—a hall, parlor, and dining room—probably were papered. The upstairs rooms—a sewing room and two

bedrooms—may have been papered, but it is likely that they were simply painted. The house's sawn-wood floors were covered, probably with ingrain or Brussels carpet, and there is a fireplace in every room.

After Clara Barkley Dorr moved out of the house in 1895, it served for a time as a residence and a private school. From 1904 until 1952, it was owned by the Edward Miller family. The house then changed hands a number of times and was sold in 1965 to the Pensacola Heritage Foundation, which began restoration. It was purchased by the Historic Pensacola Preservation Board in 1975 and is maintained as a house museum. The house's furnishings evoke the period when it was new, although only one side chair, a straight-backed Renaissance revival side chair, belonged to the Dorr family.

*The Dorr House, 311 S. Adams St. in Pensacola, is part of Historic Pensacola Village. Hours are 10 a.m. to 4 p.m. Monday through Saturday. Admission is charged. For further information, call (850) 595-5985.*

# Julee Cottage

*Pensacola*

The simple, tin-roofed Julee Cottage was built in Pensacola between 1804 and 1808 as a functional, one-and-a-half-story house sided and shingled with cypress. It belonged to the legendary Julee Panton, a "free woman of color" who is said to have tried to purchase the freedom of her fellow enslaved blacks and to have helped them in their new lives as free men and free women. Such stories can't be proven, but Julee Panton is a symbol of courage and altruism nonetheless.

It is known that the small (about twenty-seven feet by thirty-three feet) rectangular dwelling was the first of several purchases of land Panton made in Pensacola. She later sold the property to another free woman, Angelica, who went on to sell it to other black families.

Aside from its historical importance, the house is noteworthy because it is Pensacola's only surviving example of "to the sidewalk" construction. As such, it is reminiscent of the Creole cottages in the French Quarter of New Orleans. It is assumed that each of the house's double-hung windows once had single shutters.

Originally, it stood with its narrow side parallel to Zaragoza Street, and was raised on brick piers to allow air to circulate below the building. The main, or east, entrance was reached by climbing a wooden staircase, and a porch and ramp were at the rear entrance.

Inside, two identical fireplaces stand back to back in two rooms, their wooden mantels featuring a simple classical design and their hearths made of concrete. The central chimney is of beige bricks and has a flaring, corbeled cap. Crude stairs lead to a loft. Floors throughout the house are of unpainted boards.

The house stood at 214 W. Zaragoza Street for more than a century and a half until it was moved to 210 E. Zaragoza Street. It was in ruinous condition when it was moved to its present location, and it has been rehabilitated to its original, early nineteenth-century appearance. It is used as a museum of black history.

*Julee Cottage, 210 E. Zaragoza Street, is part of Historic Pensacola Village. Hours are 10 a.m. to 3:30 p.m. Monday through Saturday. Admission is charged. For further information, call (850) 595-5985.*

The Quina House, at 204 S. Alcaniz Street, is also part of Historic Pensacola Village. This one-and-a-half-story shingled frame cottage, built around 1810 by Desiderio Quina, is one of Pensacola's oldest houses still standing on its original site.

# Orman House

## *Apalachicola*

∂ᴓ

One of the more unusual aspects of Orman House is the interest it sparks in very different admirers, and the fact their interests have little to do with the vernacular Greek Revival style of the antebellum residence.

Well-adapted to its Gulf coast climate, the frame structure began its existence as a four-room house on a bluff overlooking the Apalachicola River's broad estuary and bay, in 1838. It has upper and lower porches that sheltered tall windows from rain but allowed any passing breeze to enter. Even in its earliest form, assembled on site from wood that was cut to measure near Syracuse, New York, and shipped to the port city via Key West, Thomas Orman's home was a pleasant place.

There were two bedrooms upstairs and, below, a parlor and dining room. Front walls of tongue-in-groove were flush-boarded to resemble the sort of stone that would be appropriate in Orman's upstate New York home, and some of the home's framework is made of heavy cypress tree trunks joined with maritime hawsers and wooden pegs. Ornate nods to the period's dominant style are its wooden mantelpieces, molded plaster cornices, and wide heart pine floorboards; even more luxurious is the carved acanthus-leaf frieze that surmounts the deep-set paneled front door, with its broad transom and flanking sidelights that boast carved magnolia blossoms, in local homage.

Thomas, who had arrived in Apalachicola in 1836 after establishing himself as a sugar trader in New Orleans, met and married Sarah in Florida. They had a son and, later, a granddaughter named Sara, who had no children and left the house to her nephew. It was expanded around 1895, when an addition was made to the rear of the house. Today, the 3,875-square-foot structure includes oak flooring in a ground-floor bedroom, a kitchen with a cherry floor and, leading to the gracious front porch, granite steps that once were used on a cotton warehouse on Water Street. Still standing on its original site, the restored manor house now includes a pool and livery building, documents left by generations of Orman family members, and some very interesting stories from its long past.

One concerns Sarah, who during the Civil War was a fervent secessionist; the roof of her home, with its high elevation and dormers, was the staging ground for her personal involvement in the struggle. When she wanted to signal Confederate troops returning to Apalachicola on furlough that there were Union soldiers in town, she was known to drag a large keg to the roof. The other legend about Orman House is the sort that such historic places often suggest, though researchers are adamant about this one: that it is haunted. In a series of images posted on the Internet, self-appointed ghost

hunters point out orbs that float mysteriously in digital images.

Still, it is the beauty and fine adaptation of the Greek Revival style in an early form of pre-fabricated construction that make Orman House so distinctive and enduring as a monument. It was the scene of many business and social gatherings, as Orman was a successful cotton merchant who gave the industry a major boost, making Apalachicola one of the most important exporting ports on the Gulf coast from the 1840s to the 1870s. His home won the Florida Trust for Historic Preservation Award in 1997, for outstanding restoration, and the Division of Historic Resources Florida Master Site file identifies it as a "significant state and local level example of typical early Florida prosperity and vernacular Greek Revival architecture in Florida."

*The Orman House State Park, located at 177 5th Street in Apalachicola, is open 9 a.m. to 5 p.m. Thursday through Monday. For fees and information, visit www.floridastateparks.org/ormanhouse or call (850) 653-1209.*

# Eden House

## Eden State Gardens, Point Washington

The two-story, Greek Revival–style house at Eden State Gardens near Fort Walton Beach was built by lumber baron William Henry Wesley in 1896 for his bride, Katie Strickland. According to legend, it is a replica of an antebellum mansion Wesley stayed in while on the way home from the Civil War, and indeed it does resemble the well-known Dunleith in Natchez, Mississippi. But the Wesley residence was, in fact, modeled after the Strickland family home just down the street. It had eight rooms. The Wesleys needed all of them—they had nine children.

In typical nineteenth-century style, the rooms are of equal size and arranged symmetrically on each floor. Two of the high-ceilinged rooms open off a central hall on each side of the house. In each room, four windows that stretch almost from floor to ceiling offer light and cooling cross-ventilation.

The house was built of native yellow pine, which was cut nearby and floated down the Choctawhatchee River, and stands on piers that protect the house from flooding and also increase the air circulation. The verandas show the adaptation of the Greek Revival style to Florida's climate.

When the Wesleys lived in their house, it stood in the midst of a busy lumber mill and outbuildings. Orange groves were planted so close to the house that the Wesley children could lean from the railing of the second-story porch and pick fruit. But a series of freezes killed the trees, the mill burned, and, by the 1930s, the Wesleys had converted the upstairs bedrooms into apartments. In 1953, after the death of Katie Wesley, the property was bought by a retired real estate developer.

By the time Lois Maxon bought the house in 1963, the vandalized structure was dilapidated. She renovated it, removing a wall between two ground-floor rooms and adding air conditioning, indoor plumbing, and the landscaped gardens that surround its centuries-old live oaks. Maxon named her mansion Eden and filled it with antiques, most from her family and some as old as the trees outside. Most of those pieces are still in the house.

She donated the property to the state in 1968. Among the house's highlights are the American Empire furniture in the library, the seventeenth-century canopy bed in the Blue Room, and the ornate Victorian bed in the Red Room.

*Guided tours of Eden State Gardens, four miles east of the junction of U.S. Highways 98 and 331 in Point Washington, are conducted hourly between 9 a.m. and 4 p.m. Thursdays through Mondays. Admission is charged. For details, call (850) 231-4214.*

# Gregory House

## Torreya State Park, Bristol

The two-story Gregory House originally stood at the Ocheesee Landing on the Apalachicola River. It was built by planter Jason Gregory in 1849, not long after the territory became a state and the last Seminole War ended.

The clean, classical lines of the Greek Revival structure reflect the dominant style of the period more than they do the climate of Florida, although its shutters, cedar shingled roof, interior chimneys, and columned breezeway were practical features.

The eight-room house was built of yellow pine and cypress, and sat on five-foot-high brick pillars that protected it from flooding and provided cooling ventilation. Its separate kitchen and dining room are connected by a covered walkway and stand about twenty feet from the house. Other buildings overlooking a large lawn on the original property were the warehouse on the river, a steamboat landing, a cotton gin, and houses for slaves.

The primary crop produced by Gregory's extensive holdings was cotton, and the plantation was well established by 1851. It prospered until the Civil War ended, and the abolition of slavery toppled the South's slave-based economy. Gregory, like many other planters, went bankrupt. He lost the entire plantation after the war and moved with his family to Gainesville. Not long afterward, he was able to buy the plantation house back, and his youngest daughter lived in it from about 1900 until her death in 1916. After that, it stood neglected until 1935, when it was given to the state. It was dismantled in 1935 and moved over the next three years by the Civilian Conservation Corps to its present site in Torreya State Park.

The house is now decorated with furnishings that date from about 1800 to 1900. Among the historically significant pieces are the bedroom suite that belonged to Gregory's daughter and a variety of Victorian objects.

Like the house, the park site itself is historically significant, as it was settled long ago by the state's Native Americans. In 1818, Gen. Andrew Jackson crossed the river with troops here during an Indian uprising. And the first government road built after Florida became a territory in 1821 met the river at this point.

*Tours of the Gregory House, in Torreya State Park near Route 2 in Bristol, are given at 10 a.m. Monday through Friday; 10 a.m., 2 p.m., and 4 p.m. on Saturday, Sunday, and state holidays. Admission is charged. For further information, call (904) 643-2674.*

# Maclay House

*Alfred B. Maclay State Gardens, Tallahassee*

The frame house in the vast, landscaped Alfred B. Maclay State Gardens was originally a hunting lodge. Built around 1909 by an earlier owner of the property, the 3,386-square-foot cypress house was renovated by Maclay, a wealthy New Yorker who had bought it in 1923 as a winter hideaway. He improved the house immediately, introducing such fine features as a bird's-eye-cypress paneled library and a Tiffany leaded-glass lamp.

The one-story Maclay house is of a simple, comfortable design that is well suited to its climate and purpose. It is located above Lake Hall, so that visitors see the lake across a vista of rolling lawn dotted by magnificent old growth pines. The roof curves upward slightly over the arch of the front door's fanlight, and wide side lights flank the door. To each side of the entrance are two casement windows with shutters. There are four fireplaces in the house.

Inside, the house appears today much as it did when it was occupied by Maclay and his wife Louise. The library floor is made of eighteen-inch-wide long-leaf yellow pine cut and milled on the property. A large, part-silk Tabriz carpet lies on the pine planks. Among the room's furnishings are two Chippendale roundabout chairs from about 1770 and replicas of the Mycenaean Vaphio Cups. In the living room are Chinese vases, an eighteenth-century American blanket chest, Chinese metal paintings, and an antique "Betty," or whaler's, lamp. A Persian rug covers much of the floor, which is made of quarter-cut red oak and is made to look as if it had been pegged.

The furniture in the hallway and dining room also are antiques. Among them are a Hepplewhite mahogany half-rounded dining table with tapered legs, an Early American china cabinet made of cherry, and pieces of eighteenth-century American crockery. A bedroom has been converted into a gallery in which interpretive exhibits on camellias and other plants that grow on the garden's twenty-eight acres of formal gardens are shown.

During the winter months, when plants are continuously in bloom, the gardens are well worth visiting as well. As he worked on the house, Maclay also began developing the gardens. His first effort, the Walled Garden, was created between 1923 and 1935 and features a sixteenth-century della Robbia terra-cotta sculpture and the sculpted century plant fountain that anchors a small round pool. The reflection pool, constructed between 1935 and 1944, is lined on either side with tall sabal palms. The pond that was built around 1943 mirrors the azalea beds on the hillside.

Maclay died in 1944, but Louise continued his work until 1953, when she donated the property to the state so that it could be maintained for the public as Maclay had envisioned it. The property is listed on the National Register of Historic Places.

*The Maclay house is open from January 1 through April 30 each year, to visitors of the Alfred B. Maclay Gardens State Park, 3540 Thomasville Road in Tallahassee. The gardens are open year-round, seven days a week from 9 a.m. to 5 p.m. Admission is charged. For further information, call (850) 487-4556.*

# Beadel House

*Tallahassee*

The Beadel House, the two-story frame house at Tall Timbers Research Station & Land Conservancy, near Tallahassee, represents an important period in north Florida history. The house was built and used when vast areas that had once been cotton plantations in north Florida and south Georgia were purchased by wealthy Northerners who were avid hunters. They managed their properties as quail hunting plantations. The Gilded Age economy that produced the residence is gone, but the house stands as a reminder of those days.

The original section of the house was built around 1895 by Edward Beadel, a New York businessman who came south every winter to hunt. He had purchased the land from the owners of a larger estate in Leon County and named the estate Hickory Hill Plantation.

The original two-story section is a rectangular building with a gabled roof built for $3,000 by a Thomasville contractor. Four rooms on each floor are divided by a wide central hall and staircase. There was also a kitchen that stood apart from the main house. The wide front porch offers a magnificent view of Lake Iamonia.

The home's second owner was Henry Beadel, Edward's nephew, also from New York. Henry had visited his uncle at Hickory Hill every winter during the hunting season since he was a boy. In 1919, he and his wife Genevieve purchased the property from Edward and became permanent residents of Florida. The Beadels changed the name of the property to Tall Timbers. They added a one-story, five-bay wing to the east of the older building in 1921, retaining its pleasant vernacular colonial revival style and linking the two buildings with a long porch framed with square posts, wooden balustrade, and wisteria trellis. A three-bay dormer was constructed in the old shingled roof to add more bedroom space, and the kitchen was joined to the main structure.

Painted yellow with white trim, like the main house, the 1921 addition has a master bedroom, bathroom, and a large living room. The living room is maintained as a museum that contains books, photographic equipment, and tools used for research and collecting by Henry Beadel. The room is paneled in red gum wood. Heavy oak beams support its twelve-foot-high ceiling. A seven-foot-wide fireplace dominates the north wall of the thirty-six-by-forty-foot room, and mounted fish and beehives hang from the walls. It also contains a built-in area under the east windows, where Henry worked on his special projects, such as building boats and special photography mounts for his many cameras. A keen observer of natural history, Beadel developed into a very fine wildlife photographer. He also made 16mm movies, many of which were preserved and are still at Tall Timbers today.

The house is set on brick piers with cinder-block infill on a slope facing Lake Iamonia, screened by live oaks and

magnolias. An early photo shows it with a huge front lawn, landscaped with native grasses and framed by pines and hardwood trees. Photos from early in the twentieth century show the house with a picket fence, planted flowers, a vegetable garden, and imported palm trees. Today, an open vista with period plantings is maintained at the house. The roses, daylilies and circular brick pond of Genevieve Beadel's front garden have been restored.

The main house was modernized after Mr. Beadel's death for administrative offices and lodging for research staff, although the addition had been kept as it was when the Beadels lived there. In the 1980s, the house was restored with funds from the Florida Department of State to its original interior appearance. The first floor now serves as a museum with interpretive exhibits.

Administrative offices are located on the second floor. Recognizing its historical significance, Tall Timbers was listed on the National Register of Historic Places in 1989 as one of Florida's historic cultural landscapes.

Henry Beadel was a sportsman, naturalist and conservationist. He was Secretary of the Cooperative Quail Study and an advocate for the use of fire to maintain the open, piney woods for quail and other fire-dependent species in the region. At the end of his life Beadel was a widower with no children. In 1958, he bequeathed his entire estate to be used as an ecological research station for long-term study of fire ecology and wildlife and timber management. He died in November of 1963, but his legacy lives on at Tall Timbers.

*The Beadel House at Tall Timbers is located on County Road 12 north of Tallahassee. The house is open for tours on the third Sunday of each month or by special arrangement. Tours begin at 2:15 p.m. Check the Tall Timbers web site, www.talltimbers.org, for tour dates and directions. No admission is charged. For further information, call (850) 893-4143, ext. 236.*

# The Columns
## Tallahassee

The oldest surviving house in Tallahassee, The Columns was begun in 1830 for banker William Williams, his wife, and their ten children. The three-story brick mansion was designed with an attached, two-story ell and keynote columns supporting a two-story porch and pediment.

The Williamses moved back to Georgia in 1833, however, and for ten years their house was owned by and operated as a bank. During the 1840s, banking in the state collapsed and the house was sold at a sheriff's sale in 1847 to satisfy creditors.

Eventually, the house became Mrs. Demilly's Boarding House. The structure was poorly maintained until after the Civil War, when Dr. Alexander Hawkins purchased it. He lived and conducted his practice in the porticoed Greek Revival house for more than twenty years. In 1897, it was bought by Thomas J. Roberts, one of Leon County's most successful post-war planters, for his young wife. She gave the already venerable house its name.

In 1907, The Columns was extensively restored. Almost a century old, it retained its residential character until 1925. Then, in the hands of real estate dealers, it became a center of business activity. Its basement became offices and the upper floors apartments. One of the best known of its tenants was the Dutch Kitchen, a tearoom that occupied the basement from 1925 to 1956.

The Columns was sold to the First Baptist Church in 1956, and in 1970 the church offered the building to anyone who would move it. The next year, the old house was moved to another downtown location and was renovated to serve as the headquarters of the Tallahassee Area Chamber of Commerce.

Its exterior appearance has been retained, and some rooms are furnished in a period style. The entrance hall and reception room feature antiques from about 1830 to 1845, among them the Empire mahogany mirror and the French restoration pier table. Over a red velvet sofa in the reception area is a portrait of Mrs. Benjamin Chaires, an early resident of The Columns, and other small pictures in the room are hand-colored engravings that date from 1790 to 1817. The boardroom contains two authentic late Empire chests and a large banquet table and twelve chairs in the Hepplewhite style.

*The Columns, 100 N. Duval Street in Tallahassee, is open from 8:30 a.m. to 5 p.m. Monday through Friday. No admission is charged. For further information, call (904) 224-8116.*

# Goodwood Museum and Gardens

## Tallahassee

The Tallahassee mansion and grounds are living testaments to the state's history, reaching back to the thirty-six-square-mile tract presented to French General Lafayette in 1825, soon after Florida became a territory.

But the Revolutionary War hero never visited Tallahassee, and soon began selling off his holdings. Among them were the 640 acres purchased in 1833 by North Carolina planter and naturalist Hardy Croom, discoverer of the rare torreya tree. Before he and his family died in the wreck of the steamship *Home* on the way to their new Florida home, in 1837, Croom had amassed 2,500 acres in Leon County.

His brother, Bryan Croom, inherited the property and began construction in 1839 on the two-story Georgian-style stucco mansion that was completed in the early 1840s—and that became the focus of a long-lasting lawsuit by the family of his sister-in-law. By the time the case was settled, in 1857, the Old Croom Mansion—or Goodwood, so named for its lush plantings—rose above a prosperous corn and cotton plantation.

That's when a long list of prominent owners began their residencies and, each in his or her way, improvements. The first was Arvah Hopkins, the prominent Tallahassee merchant who married the daughter of former Florida governor John Branch. His widow sold the then-160-acre property in

1885 to Dr. William Lamb Arrowsmith, an Englishman. According to legend, he was a soldier of fortune and brought lavish Italian treasures to the mansion. Arrowsmith died soon after moving to Goodwood, but his widow established the West Lawn's bulb gardens and other additions that converted the former plantation into a country estate.

After Mrs. Arrowsmith's death, in 1911, northern socialite Fanny Tiers, who was said to be one of the world's wealthiest women at the time, purchased the estate and launched further extensive renovations, which set the character of Goodwood as a prime example of the Country Estate era. Among the changes Mrs. Tiers made were the new cupola on the main house, modeled after the one at Mount Vernon, large carriage house and stables, and additions to the gardens.

In 1925, the property passed to another leading family. State Senator William C. Hodges, again according to legend, had wanted to give his wife an antique bed she had admired at Goodwood; he ended up buying the whole estate. The Hodges' additions include the aviary, that housed the senator's macaws. The couple also continued the long tradition of entertaining social and political luminaries at Goodwood. The senator died in 1940, but his widow continued to lavish care on the home; she remarried in 1948 and, after her death thirty years later, her widower, Thomas Hood, set

up the Margaret E. Wilson Foundation in her memory. In 1989 it began overseeing the restoration of the historic home, gardens, and outbuildings.

Key attractions at Goodwood are the guest house, where the Crooms lived while their mansion was being constructed; the old kitchen, an outbuilding that once served the main house; the Old Garden Roses, antique specimens that bloom between March and May; the Goodwood "dogs," sculptural figures that have "guarded" the entrance to the main house since the 1840s; eight marble fireplaces; a winding mahogany staircase; and Fanny Tiers's cupola, which floods the attic and grand staircase with light and draws hot air upward to be vented.

*Goodwood Museum and Gardens, located at 1600 Miccosukee Road in Tallahassee, is open for tours 10 a.m. to 4 p.m. Monday through Friday, 10 a.m. to 2 p.m. Saturday. For fees and more information, visit www.taltrust.org/goodwood or call (850) 877-4202.*

# Knott House Museum
## Tallahassee

*"The House that Rhymes"*

There are many distinctive qualities about the antebellum Knott House in Tallahassee. The gracious two-story mansion was built in 1843 by a free African-American man, George Proctor, and later became the home of the patron of the state's first black physician, William Gunn. Its historical significance increased with the years. At the end of the War Between the States, the Tallahassee house became the headquarters of Union General Edward McCook. The slaves of north Florida were freed by a proclamation read from the mansion's front steps on May 20, 1865, a day still celebrated in many Panhandle communities as "Emancipation Day."

But it was only after the house became the property of its most prominent owners, William and Luella Knott, that the frame house earned the nickname it would keep, and that would charm visitors: the sweet sobriquet of "The House that Rhymes."

In 1928, William was returning to Tallahassee and the position of state treasurer, after a decade serving as

director of Florida's mental-health hospital. Knott came back to Tallahassee on the eve of the devastating New York stock market crash and the ensuing Great Depression. During the 1930s, he became one of Florida's most influential politicians, handling finances and implementing New Deal legislation.

He became the state's first auditor, its comptroller, and its treasurer. His wife was also politically active, working tirelessly toward temperance, keeping the sale of alcohol banned for more than fifty years in Tallahassee. Even more enduring, though, was her contribution to the state's historical treasures.

Luella Knott filled her new old home with cherished Victorian-era furnishings and, drawing on her talents as a musician and

writer (best known for her text on Christian living), she composed poems to her antiques. Those poems are still attached by ribbons to their inspirations: floor lamps, teapots, chairs, chests, gilded mirrors. To one such mirror, she penned her lyrical thoughts: "When you look in me, do I reflect, What your ego SHOULD expect?"

A more reflective lyric was attached to another of her gilded mirrors: "Look at me from near and far, And I will tell you what you are; Should the picture be complete, You wouldn't have so much conceit." A chair inscription reads, "Grandmother's chair could have no arms, For when she sat, she spread. If she should dare use Grandpa's chair, Her hoops would hit her head."

The blend of history and personality at Knott House sets it apart from many other historic homes, as does its placement at an unusual time: the late 1920s. It certainly is linked to key events in the state's long history; just as decidedly Knott House was a real home, a distinctive time capsule that captures a specific owner and moment. And so it remains. As one of Louella's poems says: "Where do we go to have some fun? East Park Avenue, 3-0-1."

*Knott House Museum, 301 E. Park Avenue in Tallahassee (corner of Park Avenue and Calhoun Street), offers free public tours on the hour on Wednesday–Friday from 1 p.m. to 3 p.m. and on Saturday from 10 a.m. to 3 p.m. Group tours at other times by appointment for $1.00 per person. Closed during August. For further information, call (850) 922-2459.*

# Bellevue

## Tallahassee

The trim, one-and-a-half-story frame Murat House was the home of Catherine Willis Murat, widow of Prince Achille Murat. He was the exiled Prince of Naples and a nephew of Napoleon Bonaparte, and she was a great-grandniece of George Washington. During the second French Empire, after Murat's death, Catherine Murat was officially recognized as a princess and given financial assistance by Napoleon III, whose court she visited. Yet the Murat house is a humble one.

Murat's widow purchased the house in 1854. She called the house Bellevue—French for "lovely vista"—and lived in it until her death in 1867. It originally sat on 520 acres about two miles west of Tallahassee on the Jackson Bluff Road. The Murat house was moved to its present location in southwest Tallahassee in 1967, and its interior was restored to the period when the princess lived there. It is furnished with such mid-nineteenth-century pieces as a washstand with ewer and basin in the bedroom, a late Empire-style pier table in the hallway, and a Hepplewhite corner cabinet in the parlor.

The charming frame structure shows the fine adjustment of Florida vernacular architecture to its environment and climate. Chimneys rise from each end of the cottage, which has porches on each façade. Those porches are covered by the roof, which projects over the open sections of the house. The house itself is raised above the ground on brick piers. Tall windows on three sides of the house offer cross-ventilation, and the steep pitch of the shingled roof allows hot air to rise to the top of the ceiling, leaving the lower part of the house cool.

*Bellevue is on the grounds of the Tallahassee Museum at 3945 Museum Drive in Tallahassee. Hours are 9 a.m. to 5 p.m. Monday through Saturday, 12:30 p.m. to 5 p.m. Sunday. Admission is charged. For further information, call (850) 576-1636.*

# Cracker House

*Forest Capital State Park, Perry*

The restored pioneer Cracker House is similar to many houses built in the Panhandle soon after Florida became a territory in the early nineteenth century. Settlers moved south from South Carolina, Virginia, and Georgia. Those newcomers came in ox-drawn wagons, cracking their whips over the heads of their animals, a practice which, according to legend, caused them to be dubbed Crackers. Unable to build with their accustomed clay, they adapted their building styles to a new material—the abundant lumber they found in north Florida.

A typical Cracker house, this one-story cabin in Forest Capital State Park near Perry was built around 1863 by Wiley Washington Whiddon. It was made with double-notched square logs cut from his land. The house is sixty feet long and consists of four rooms—a living room and a kitchen/dining room separated by a breezeway (called a dogtrot) and two bedrooms, one for boys and one for girls, that were added later. The house's shake shingles were made from cedar, and its longer beams were lap-jointed and held together with wooden pegs. A wooden fence surrounded this pioneer home, keeping the chickens in and foxes and other predators out. The yard was always carefully raked to allow the occupants to see snakes more readily and to protect against fire. Porches on both sides of the building offered shade and shelter from showers, allowing the large windows to be kept open to admit breezes. The house was raised from the ground so that cooling air could flow beneath it.

All rooms in the Cracker House have fireplaces with chimneys made of fieldstone and homemade mortar. The house has such period furnishings as mosquito netting that flows from the ceiling in a pyramid over the bed, simple chairs and tables, and, outside, a cane grinder and a hand-wringer. Also on the grounds are a vineyard, stable, henhouse, and general-purpose shed.

The Cracker House, at the Forest Capital State Museum, is about a mile south of Perry on U.S. Highways 27 and 19. The park is open 9 a.m. to noon and 1 p.m. to 5 p.m. Thursday through Monday. Admission is charged. For further information, call (904) 584-3227.

# II
# St. Augustine and Northeast Florida

Victorian House,
St. Augustine

## St. Augustine and Northeast Florida

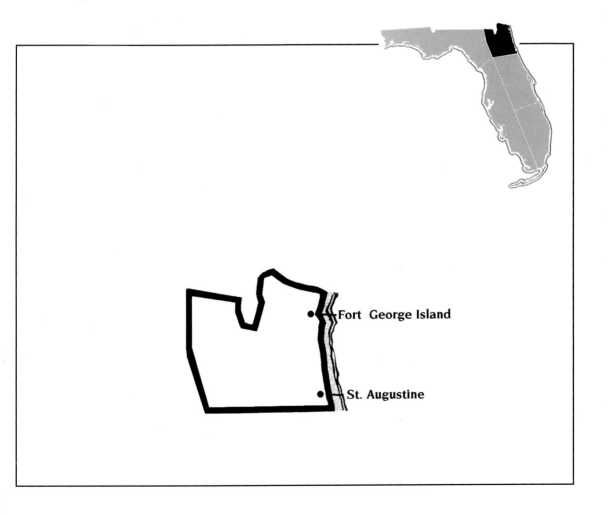

Fort George Island

St. Augustine

# The Spanish Legacy

Although English and Native American influences can be found in the historic buildings of northeastern Florida, the dominant early influence was Spanish. That is hardly surprising, because the first Spanish explorers to set foot in the new colony, Pascua Florida, did so somewhere near present-day Ponte Vedra Beach, south of Jacksonville Beach, in 1513. The Spanish dominated the region for centuries.

When Pedro Menéndez de Avilés established St. Augustine in 1565, he and his men probably built dwellings like those of the Native Americans in the area—using palm thatch and wood, or perhaps wattle and daub. They built a series of log forts to defend their settlement until the late seventeenth century, when work began on the sturdy, thick-walled Castillo de San Marcos. Local coquina stone was the building material.

When construction began on the fort in 1672, residents of St. Augustine also began using coquina or a combination of coquina stone and tabby—a primitive mortar made of crushed shells, limestone, sand, and water—on their homes. Most houses, however, still were made of wood.

Many of the town's more perishable wooden houses were destroyed in 1702, when English colonists from the Carolinas attacked St. Augustine. In the building boom that followed, the Spanish settlers built houses that were more permanent and fireproof. By 1763, when Spain ceded Florida to England in the Treaty of Paris, St. Augustine was a bustling town with three thousand inhabitants and a number of stone, or stone-and-wood, houses.

The new British inhabitants of St. Augustine, in need of firewood, tore down many of the flimsy wooden structures and expanded the existing stone structures. They usually added fireplaces to rooms formerly warmed by braziers, and glass to windows that had been shuttered or latticed but not glazed. British occupation lasted only twenty years, but the improvements during that time endured and created a unique architectural style still seen throughout the Ancient City.

Prosperity came to the region in the early years of the nineteenth century, when Florida became first a territory and then a state. By mid-century, St. Augustine was a thriving community. The arrival of a honeymooning Henry Flagler in 1883 increased its popularity among winter tourists, many of them invalids eager to rest quietly among the city's fragrant gardens and groves. They came south and stayed all winter at hotels like that operated by Louisa Maria Philipa Fatio.

During the 1880s, however, Flagler determined that he would make the area a booming resort. He built the grand Ponce de Leon Hotel and the nearby Alcazar, and acquired and renovated the Cordova. He provided the town easy access to the rest of the nation by rail.

Within little more than a decade of the opening of the Ponce de Leon, Flagler and his fashionable tourists moved on to the more stylish Palm Beach, and then on to warmer Miami. St. Augustine and neighboring cities grew gradually, and never failed to attract sightseers and visitors.

Peña-Peck House
St. Augustine

# Kingsley Plantation

*Fort George Island, Jacksonville*

The state's oldest surviving plantation house was built under the direction of John McQueen and completed in 1798. By then, the island was cleared for growing Sea Island cotton, valued for its long silky fibers. McQueen received the one-thousand-acre plantation, located on Fort George Island, as a land grant from the Spanish government in 1791.

The plantation's second owner, John Houston McIntosh, purchased the plantation in 1804 and, for ten years, McIntosh ran it successfully. In 1812, he became the leader of a plot known as the Patriots Rebellion to overthrow the Spanish government in order to make Florida a United States Territory. When the rebellion failed, McIntosh left Florida. He rented the Fort George plantation to Zephaniah Kingsley in 1814; the new tenant purchased the island in 1817 for $7,000.

Zephaniah Kingsley moved his family to Fort George Island and rebuilt the plantation. While the plantation house remained standing, many of its outbuildings and the slave quarters were burned during the Patriots Rebellion. With an enslaved work force of about sixty, the Fort George plantation produced Sea Island cotton. Kingsley's slaves also grew the provisions needed for the plantation, raised livestock, and fished in the rivers surrounding the plantation.

He brought his wife and three children to the plantation (their fourth was born there). His wife, Anna Madgigine Jai, was from Senegal, Africa, and had been purchased by Kingsley as a slave. She actively participated in plantation management, acquiring her own land and slaves after being freed in 1811.

Kingsley was a large landholder and slave owner in Florida, acquiring over thirty-two thousand acres and two hundred slaves between 1803 and his death in 1843. Once Florida became a United States territory in 1821, Kingsley was appointed to the Second Legislative Council of the Territory of Florida under James Monroe. He advocated maintaining a class system in Florida, composed of slaves, free blacks, and free whites.

Kingsley believed that slavery was necessary for the Southern economy, and that the class system would promote efficiency and reduce the threat of slave insurrection. His pleas were ignored, and over the next two decades, laws were enacted that severely restricted the civil liberties of free blacks. Frustrated that his words were rejected, and to escape what he called a "spirit of intolerant prejudice," Kingsley moved his family to Haiti, the only free black republic in the hemisphere, in 1837. There Kingsley established a colony for his family and some of his former slaves. He sold the plantation

to his nephew, Kingsley Beatty Gibbs, who managed the plantation for ten years. After Gibbs, there were several planters who tried, often unsuccessfully, to make a profit at Fort George. After the Civil War, the island was sold to John Rollins, who remodeled the kitchen and plantation house.

Originally, the plantation house included a basement, the two-story center section, and four pavilion rooms, one on each corner off the two story center section. The post–Civil War house includes an additional two rooms, bay windows, an indoor staircase, and the walkway between the main house and the kitchen house. Rollins also enlarged many of the windows and removed several fireplaces from the building.

Today, visitors can explore Florida's plantation history by touring the grounds, which include the plantation house, kitchen house, barn, and slave quarters.

*Kingsley Plantation is a part of the National Park Service's Timucuan Ecological and Historic Preserve and is open daily, except for Thanksgiving Day, Christmas Day, and New Year's Day. Admission is free. For further information, call 904-251-3537 or visit www.nps. gov/timu.*

# Casa de Solana

## St. Augustine

Completed in 1763 for wealthy native St. Augustinian Don Manuel Solana, the two-and-a-half-story coquina structure in St. Augustine was converted into a bed-and-breakfast hotel in 1982. Its style and materials make it a typical, if grand, St. Augustine building, with its *balcon de la calle,* or street balcony, projecting from its second story and its use of local stone.

Solana, a descendant of the first white settler born in America, chose to stay in St. Augustine after 1763, when Florida was ceded to England by Spain in the Treaty of Paris. After most of the city's Spanish residents fled to Cuba, Solana remained to settle real estate claims. He married in 1777, and had eighteen children with his wife, who was fourteen years old when they married. Solana died in 1825, one of St. Augustine's wealthiest citizens.

His house—said to be the seventh-oldest in the city—reflects his prominence as it also reflects the city's architectural heritage. It combines coquina, a locally quarried shell stone, with wood—in this case hand-pegged pine floors and hand-hewn yellow pine joists that run the depth of the structure to support the balconies. Unlike many of St. Augustine's historic homes, which evolved from simple wooden or tabby modules, Solana's twenty-one-room house was a noteworthy residence from the start: it had English-style fireplaces built into the walls rather than the braziers the Spanish settlers were accustomed to placing in the center of the room. The floor plan, however, was purely Spanish, with the entrance opening into the gentleman's living room and

each room opening into another.

Sturdy beams were left exposed in many rooms, and fine paneling lined some walls. Windows were large, deep-seated, and paned with glass in the English fashion. Hearths were made of marble. Much of the house remains as it was. A porch was enclosed to create a foyer, and some downstairs floors are now tiled. The original nineteenth-century paneling remains, and the home is furnished with eighteenth-century English antiques.

*Casa de Solana is at 21 Aviles Street in St. Augustine. For further information, call (904) 824-3555.*

# Fernandez-Llambias House

## St. Augustine

The two-story, hip-roof house on St. Francis Street in St. Augustine was built during the first Spanish colonial period, sometime before 1763. When new, the dwelling probably was a one-story structure that had walls of native limestone or coquina. The second story was probably added while the British ruled Florida, between 1763 and 1783. When the region was ceded to England, the small stone house belonged to Pedro Fernandez.

Then, as now, its floors were made of tabby, a primitive mortar made of crushed shellstone, lime, sand, and water—and its wooden parts were of yellow pine. The second story continued the simple lines of the first, but the front and rear balconies that were added with the new upper level provide shade, protection from showers, and cooling breezes that circulate through the house.

During the second period of Spanish rule, from 1783 to 1821, the expanded house belonged to Juan Andreu, the first of several owners of Minorcan descent. The Minorcans had come to America in 1777 to colonize a British community called New Smyrna, and when that plan failed, many moved to St. Augustine. The Andreu family owned the coquina house until Florida became a territory of the United States, in 1821. Soon afterward it became the home of Peter and Joseph Manucy. In 1854, the Manucys sold

the house to Catalina Llambias, and his family lived there for the next sixty-five years.

The house was occupied until 1954, when the typically St. Augustine structure was restored to the territorial period of about 1821 to 1845 by members of the St. Augustine Restoration and Preservation Association. Some of its interior walls retain the many layers of paint applied to them over the years, while others reveal the lathing-and-shingling techniques used in the house's construction.

Among noteworthy furnishings are a drop-leaf table and chair set that are reproductions of originals made in Minorca for the house, an image of Nuestra Señora de Monto Toro, patroness of Minorca, spirit lamps, rugs, and a small table that once

belonged to the Llambias family. The upstairs bedrooms are furnished with English, Spanish, and Early American pieces from that period.

*The Fernandez-Llambias House, at 33 St. Francis Street in St. Augustine, is open 2 p.m. to 4 p.m. on the third Sunday of each month. No admission is charged. For further information, call (904) 824-9823.*

# Peña-Peck House

## St. Augustine

The Peña-Peck House is one of three dozen Spanish Colonial buildings left in St. Augustine and one of the most significant. Built around 1749–1750 of native coquina stone, it was originally a one-story, L-shaped building with a flat roof and tabby floors. The covered loggia overlooking the garden was a unique feature and the footprint of the first floor and loggia remain unchanged today.

The first documented residents were the Spanish Royal Treasurer Juan Esteban de Peña and his wife, Maria Antonia. When Spain relinquished Florida to Britain after the Treaty of Paris, the Peñas left Florida for Cuba.

The British (1763–1784) brought changes to the house. Four fireplaces and chimneys were added along with glazed windows and the formerly separate kitchen was connected to the building at the east end. The house was then leased to the newly appointed Lt. Governor, John Moultrie. He remained in the house until 1778 and was followed by Governor Patrick Tonyn. He settled the affairs of British East Florida from this house until 1785 although the Spanish had returned and most of the British had evacuated in 1784.

After Spain regained Florida, Peña's widow tried to reclaim the house but her claim was thwarted by the Spanish government, who declared ownership because Peña had died. The house fell into disrepair, changing hands a number of times.

In 1821, Florida was purchased from Spain by the United States, opening the territory to American settlers. Dr. Seth Peck, a native of Lyme, Connecticut, arrived from upstate New York in 1833 to become the town doctor in response to an inquiry from Dr. Andrew Anderson. His wife, Sarah, and five children soon joined him, settling into Mrs. Whitehurst's boarding house, now known as the Ximenez-Fatio House on Aviles Street. In 1837, he purchased the old house, making plans for it to become his home and office. He completely renovated the structure, adding a second story of wood, including a balcony on the south end, and demolishing what was left of the east wing. Dr. Peck's medical office was on the first floor opening onto St. George Street where the Woman's Exchange gift shop is located today. The large northwest corner room opening onto Treasury Street was rented as a general store. The family occupied the second floor rooms with the kitchen and dining room remaining downstairs. The house was furnished with eighteenth- and nineteenth-century pieces brought from their former home as well as those purchased locally. These included a fine collection of European oil paintings and works by Florida artists of the nineteenth century, including Martin Johnson Heade.

Over the next ninety-five years three generations of the Peck family would

occupy the house. Today, the Peck furniture and paintings remain in the house and are on display to the public. In 1931, the last surviving family member, Miss Anna Burt, willed the property to the city of St. Augustine to be shown as "as an example of the old antebellum homes of the south." Members of the Woman's Exchange have managed, maintained, and interpreted the house since May 1932.

*The Peña-Peck House is at 143 St. George Street in St. Augustine. Hours are 10 a.m. to 4 p.m. Monday through Saturday, 10 a.m. to 4 p.m. Sunday. Admission is charged. For further information, call (904) 829-5064.*

# Raintree Restaurant

## St. Augustine

When the century-old frame home of Hattie Masters was transformed into the Raintree Restaurant in 1981, its new owners had it stripped down to the bare wood and completely restored before adding a new dining wing.

Patches of surviving tin roof were replaced on the house, which was built between 1879 and 1885. Windows, walls, brackets, and other wooden architectural elements were either restored or replaced with duplicates of the cypress originals. The new porch ceilings feature tongue-and-groove construction, just as the old ones did. All four fireplaces are in their original locations, although antique mantels from other old homes were installed on the two first-floor fireplaces.

The house's history stretches back to the days of the second Spanish period in St. Augustine. It stands on land that was given to Gen. Joseph Hernandez, Florida's first territorial delegate to Congress and the man who in 1837 captured Seminole leader Osceola under a flag of truce.

Forty years later, the land was purchased at public auction by Bernard Masters, a thirty-seven-year-old Confederate veteran who also was a prominent Minorcan rancher and real estate owner. The land was known as the Masters Tract, and the first house built on it was the Homestead. The Masterses raised their five daughters there. They added other buildings on the property, among them the building now known as the Raintree Restaurant and the identical house that once stood beside it.

In 1897, when she married St. Augustine dry-goods merchant A. J. Collins, Hattie Masters became the owner of the house at 102 San Marco Avenue. Her sister moved

into the matching house when she married, and Masters's daughters raised their children in the two trim Victorian homes. The Raintree

house, the only one of the Masters's houses still standing, became a boardinghouse for a few years at the end of the Second World War and then was converted into the first of three restaurants, the Corner House. The families that operated the first two restaurants in the old house lived on the second floor.

Today's restored Raintree Restaurant closely resembles a Victorian Florida vernacular house. Its two-story porches are ornamented with turned spindles and lacy brackets, and its crisp clapboards are painted a sunshine yellow color.

*The Raintree Restaurant is at 102 San Marco Avenue in St. Augustine. It is open 5 p.m. to 9:30 p.m. for dinner. For further information, call (904) 824-7211 or visit www. raintreerestaurant.com.*

# The Oldest House

## St. Augustine

The two-story stone and clapboard structure in the Ancient City shows several influences. Archaeology has proven that the present house stands on the site of a much older, more primitive dwelling, probably a board-and-thatch hut built in the 1600s and burned during the invasion of English troops in 1702.

By the early 1700s the current house, then a one-story structure, had been built to take the place of the more perishable hut. This house is of coquina stone, a native shellstone quarried on nearby Anastasia Island, and a tabby floor: a mixture of lime, sand, crushed shells, water, and boiled linseed oil.

The house was occupied by Tomas Gonzalez y Hernandez, a Canary Island immigrant who was an artilleryman at the Castillo de San Marcos. It is thought that he might have acquired it through his marriage in 1723 to local girl Francisca Guevara y Dominguez. The family lived in the house until 1763, when Spain exchanged Florida for Cuba, which Great Britain had captured. Most Spanish inhabitants of St. Augustine evacuated to Cuba.

In 1775, the Gonzalez's house became the property of Sergeant Major Joseph Peavett, the acting paymaster for the British garrison, and his wife Mary Evans Fenwick, a midwife. The expanded the house for use as a tavern with a clapboard second floor.

Further modernization included glass panes that replaced the latticework windows, fireplaces, and a folding partition wall that could be opened to make two rooms convert into one large assembly room. After Joseph's death in 1786, his widow continued to operate the tavern for a time with John Hudson, her new husband, a gambler whose debts forced her to sell the building at auction in 1790. It was purchased by Geronimo Alvarez, a Spaniard, and was his family's home for almost a century. He was the first "Alcalde Ordinario"—the mayor of St. Augustine under the liberal Spanish constitution of 1812. His son Antonio, who inherited the house, was also mayor during the American Territorial Period.

With the destruction of another house during the Civil War, the old Alvarez home took the title of "Oldest House" in Florida. By 1892, Dr. C. P. Carver, then-owner, began charging to enter his home "to discourage visitors." The house became the headquarters of the St. Augustine Historical Society in 1918 and in the 1950s was restored to its late-eighteenth-century appearance. A roofed balcony projects from the east end of the structure and cypress-shake shingles cover its hip roof.

Inside, some of the rooms are furnished in the plain Spanish style of the 1700s, while others show the influences of later styles. Mary Peavett's room reflects the time

it was used—the late eighteenth century. The bed of General Hernandez, a leader in the Second Seminole War, may be seen in one bedroom, which is furnished in the style of the American Territorial Period.

The reconstructed kitchen, in the style so typical of Spanish buildings and hot-climate dwellings, occupies a separate building to reduce the danger of fire and to keep cooking odors out of the main house.

*The Oldest House, located at 14 St. Francis Street in St. Augustine, is open 9 a.m. to 5 p.m. every day except Christmas. The last tour begins at 4:30 p.m. Admission is charged. For further information, call (904) 824-2872 or visit www.oldesthouse.org.*

# Victorian House

*St. Augustine*

The cream-colored, blue-trimmed Victorian House in St. Augustine was built in the mid-1880s by Albert Rogero on the site of an earlier Spanish structure.

The Rogero family, descendants of Minorcans who had fled to St. Augustine from New Smyrna a century earlier, lived in the house and rented out some of its rooms until 1904. It isn't known who owned the two-story frame house in the following thirty-plus years, but in the 1940s, the Meyers family bought it and converted it to a private home. In 1983, Daisy Morden purchased the house and opened it as a bed-and-breakfast.

The porch, which extends across the entire façade, is decorated with typically Victorian turned spindles and brackets. The downstairs rooms feature ten-foot-high ceilings, heart-pine floors, and simple crafted heart-pine woodwork. The rooms are furnished with a mixture of country Victorian antiques, among them a canopy spool cherry bed and several iron and brass beds. The walls are decorated with stenciling, and the rooms feature a collection of hand-hooked rugs, Amish quilts, woven coverlets, and early lace.

Additional buildings on the property include a carriage house and a combination kitchen and wash house that now is a potter's shop. The house is on one of St. Augustine's original residential blocks.

*Victorian House Bed and Breakfast is at 11 Cadiz Street, St. Augustine. For further information, call (904) 824-5414.*

# Westcott House

*St. Augustine*

The Victorian clapboard Westcott House in St. Augustine was built in the late 1880s for Dr. John Westcott. He was involved in the development of the St. Johns Railroad and the Intracoastal Waterway.

In 1983, it was converted into a bed-and-breakfast inn. The house has porches on its first and second stories facing the street and a smaller first-level porch around a projecting bay on the side of the house. Its double front door is to the left of the symmetrical façade. The other two bays contain large casement windows. Delicate scrollwork brackets ornament the wide eaves, their graceful lines echoing those of the scrollwork brackets on the porch's square columns.

The Westcott House is raised on piers to protect it from flooding and to permit cooling breezes to circulate below. The deep porches and tall windows also allow the house to take full advantage of the subtropical climate's every breeze; the windows are shaded by the porch and sheltered from storms.

The house is in St. Augustine's Historic District, overlooking Matanzas Bay and the Bridge of Lions.

*The Westcott House is at 146 Avenida Menendez in St. Augustine. Room rates vary at the bed-and-breakfast. For further information, call (904) 824-4301.*

# Ximenez- Fatio House

## St. Augustine

The Ximenez-Fatio House is considered to be one of St. Augustine's most significant and best preserved Spanish Colonial dwellings. It is located south of the Plaza on Aviles Street, in the oldest section of the city.

The two-story whitewashed coquina house with tabby floors and detached kitchen was built in 1798 by Andres Ximenez, a wealthy Spanish merchant who lived upstairs with his family and operated a general store and tavern on the ground floor. Margaret Cook purchased the house in the mid-1820s, added a wing of bedrooms and transformed it into a spacious boarding house, operated by Eliza Whitehurst. In turn, the house was sold to Sara Petty Anderson who enlarged the property, and later, to Louisa Fatio who ran it as a fashionable inn for twenty years (1855–1875).

In 1939, the property was purchased by The National Society of the Colonial Dames of America in the State of Florida. The Florida Dames were pioneers in recognizing the importance of rescuing historic property and have been lauded as leaders of the preservation movement in St. Augustine. The house was listed in the National Register of Historic Places in 1973. In 1976, the Ximenez-Fatio House Museum, recreated as accurately as possible, was opened to tourists, reflecting the lifestyle of an inn during the Territorial and Early Statehood periods (1821–1861).

Guests might have included military officers assigned to the fort, the local doctor, a sea captain, an artist, families seeking safe haven from the Indian uprisings, and invalids who came from the north to recuperate from consumption. All the bedrooms are appointed with amenities: wash stand, mosquito netting, and commode. Each room reflects a distinct personality defined by items belonging to the occupant.

The reputation of the house centered on its food, which was plentiful, varied, and fresh. The dining tables covered in damask are set with wineglasses, silver, and beautiful English china, identified by artifacts found on site or known to have been family pieces. The original brick beehive oven and open cooking fireplace are remarkable features of the only remaining detached kitchen in St. Augustine from the Colonial period. A magnificent old fig tree shades the kitchen service area, which includes an early 1800s wash house recreated from photographs and archaeological evidence.

Throughout the house sheer curtains grace the windows and shutters diffuse the light. Shaded porches overlook the courtyard, facing a large garden fragrant with orange trees. A visitors center offers award-winning mixed media exhibits, including the priceless circa 1650 white bronze Caravaca Cross—a rare archaeological discovery found on site in 2002.

*The Ximenez-Fatio House, 20 Aviles Street in St. Augustine, is open Tuesday through Saturday, 11:00 a.m. to 4:00 p.m. For further information, visit www.ximenezfatiohouse.org or call (904) 829-3575.*

# III
# Central Florida

The Gamble Place,
Port Orange

# Central Florida

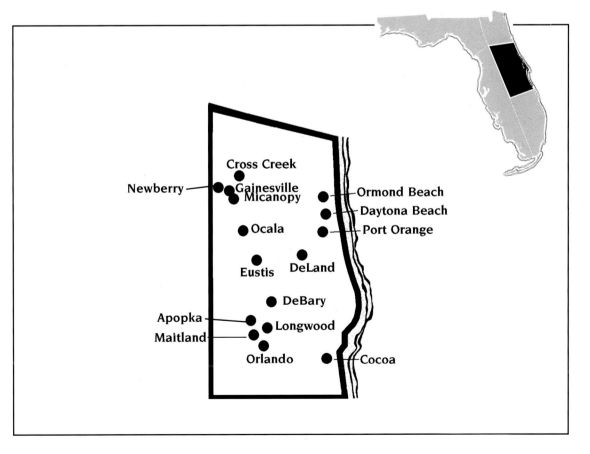

# Steamboats and Citrus Groves

Central Florida includes the areas around Orlando, Daytona Beach, Cocoa, and Gainesville. When the Spanish arrived in Florida in the sixteenth century, much of the zone was inhabited by members of the Timucuan tribe. This tribe became extinct by the 1700s, largely because of diseases contracted from whites, warfare with other tribes, and the slavery imposed by Europeans.

During the first half of the nineteenth century, most of central Florida was part of a vast, relatively undifferentiated tract known bluntly as Mosquito County. But later, Union soldiers returned home from the Civil War with tales of the region's warm, healthful climate and lush landscape.

The area's terrain varies widely, from the low-lying St. Johns River near the coast to the sandy central highlands. Although it was settled much later than St. Augustine and the Panhandle, its location between the two coasts and its navigable waterways brought people to central Florida early on.

One incursion had tragic results. On December 28, 1835, Maj. Francis Dade and 139 soldiers were marching through open pine and palmetto country near present-day Bushnell when a band of Seminoles descended on them and killed all but two. The incident led to the Second Seminole War, which ended with the near-extinction of the tribe.

The region, however, has long been associated with more pleasant memories. Soon after the Civil War, the Golden Age of Steamships began in Florida. Visitors seeking warm sun and citrus cruised along the natural waterways to such sites as Blue Spring, where the Thursby family established a landing, a home, and even a post office.

By the 1880s, when the railroads took the place of the boats and tourism was rapidly increasing, a number of central Florida cities were founded and prospered. The homes that were built in Mellonville (now Sanford), Orlando, Blue Spring, Micanopy, DeLand, and Cocoa reflect the economy and taste of each location. Yet they also show a sensitivity to the climate and dominant architectural styles, such as the high Victorian, Queen Anne, Gothic, Classical Revival, and simple vernacular Cracker.

Waterhouse
Residence, Maitland

# Dudley Farm

## Newberry

❦

Some historic homes politely invite you to enter, and then entertain you with their stories and recreations of the past. Others, chief among them the workaday homestead at Dudley Farm Historic State Park in Newberry, just west of Gainesville, thrust their guests right into the past and let them actually experience what life was like when those homes were new and still on the frontier.

The farm, which was settled in the late 1800s by Phillip Benjamin Harvey Dudley and his wife Mary Magdelina Thomson, reveals its cultural roots in the architectural style that predominated at that time in the family's hometown, Charleston, South Carolina, as well as in their adaptations to the humid climate of rural north central Florida. Tall windows are sheltered by a porch on the front of the raw board-and-batten pine structure, and the double fenestration in the dormer directly above that porch offers a pleasing repetition of its geometric form.

Simplicity and function are the keywords in the house, which Dudley purchased by land grant in 1859, two years before serving in the Civil War. It's where he and Mary raised the surviving five of their seven children, and where Philip Benjamin Harvey Dudley Jr. and his wife Sarah Fannie Wynne would later bring up a family of twelve while continuing to work the land

in traditional ways. The youngest of their children, Myrtle Elizabeth Dudley, was born in 1901; she donated the property to the state in 1983, to be preserved as a living history museum. Along with the gardens and farmhouse are eighteen historic—not reproduction—structures on the site, dating from between the mid-1880s to 1945. Among them are the functional kitchen outbuilding, hay barn, syrup shed, tobacco barn, dairy shed, stables, smokehouse, canning house, and the general store that served what gradually became a crossroads community, bypassed by the railroad.

At its heart, however, is the home, which is furnished with the family's original possessions. There are hand-stitched quilts and their large quilting frame, the 1835 Bible that P. B. H. Dudley carried through the Civil War, and photographs, along with changing exhibits that illustrate pioneer life in Newberry. When the Dudleys, progressive farmers in Charleston, reached their new homestead, they found rolling land dotted with longleaf pine and wiregrass. Wood became the material for all their buildings as well as for the split-rail fences they constructed.

The land, with its sinkholes and rich organic soil, was ideal for farming, and the Dudleys planted grape arbors, pecan and fruit trees, field peas, sweet potatoes, sugar

cane, and peanuts. They raised livestock, but also found native deer, turkeys, gopher tortoises, bats, and bluebirds thriving on their new farmstead. Dudley Farm today appears to be a close cousin of what it has been for more than 150 years: a site still occupied by original buildings. Thanks to a team of dedicated docents who provide interpretations in period costumes, it actively shares its secrets with its visitors.

*Dudley Farm Historic State Park, 18730 W. Newberry Road in Newberry, west of Gainesville, is open 9 a.m. to 5 p.m. Wednesday through Sunday. For fees and details, visit http://www.floridastateparks.org/dudleyfarm or call (352) 472-1142.*

# Haile Homestead at Kanapaha Plantation

*Gainesville*

The large house built by Thomas Evans Haile and his wife Esther Serena Chesnut Haile near Gainesville more than 150 years ago is one of the most unusual—and unusually well preserved—in Florida. The Haile Homestead still stands on its original site, on the forty-acre section of what was a fifteen-hundred-acre Sea Island cotton plantation that the couple named Kanapaha, after the pre-Columbian Timucuan village that had existed in the area.

The Hailes had moved south from Camden, South Carolina, in 1854 with their first of fifteen children. They brought with them about sixty-five slaves, who would live in eighteen buildings at Kanapaha. The 6,200-square-foot home, completed in 1856, was built by those slaves using old-growth heart pine and cypress in its braced frame construction and mortise-and-tenon joinery.

Its Cracker style provided the greatest relief from hot, humid weather and clearly reflects the early nineteenth-century Greek Revival style of the family's antebellum hometown. The classical symmetrical structure was built with hand-hewn pine framing members, set on sturdy mortared limestone piers that rise almost four feet off the ground, to allow any cooling breezes available to flow beneath the main house.

Other vernacular aspects of the homestead's architecture are the deep overhang provided by the broad porch that extends beyond the main structure's walls; twelve-foot-high ceilings; tall, wide windows with louvred shutters; and the hand-split shingles that were replaced by a galvanized metal roof in 1937. It was built by enslaved craftsmen, and one of the things that makes the structure so unique is that many of its builders are known, among them carpenters Billy Watts and Johnson Chestnut and stonemason Henry Gaines, all of whom accompanied the Hailes to Florida. In addition, a nearby family lent woodworker Ned Chisholm and his son Thomas to build its solid roof.

Another of the Haile Homestead's intriguing aspects is that it appears to be much smaller than it is; indeed, it is only when seen with a person on the porch or in the front yard for scale that it's possible to grasp the sheer size of the ten-room house. But what sets it apart most of all are the inscriptions on its interior walls, adding up to more than 12,500 words and giving it its nickname of "the talking house."

Tom and Serena Haile died in the mid-

1880s, and left the house to their fourteenth child, Evans. A prominent Gainesville attorney, he used the house for parties on the weekends and holidays, and left such documents as his Jan. 18, 1893, note: "Peace on Earth and Good Will Towards Evans Haile." Other inscriptions throughout the house feature guests' names, shopping lists, growth charts of children and grandchildren, inventories of linens and silver, business records, recipes for whitewash and flights of fancy. "If love be cold, do not despair/ there's always long underwear," reads one, while another jots down a prescription: "15 drops turpentine, 10–15 drops laudanum, 1 teaspoon paregoric in glass of water. Repeat every 3 hours if necessary." In this home—which was built by slaves, farmed by its family for decades and then allowed to decay gracefully until it was listed on the National Register of Historic Places in 1986, and finally restored in 1996—one inscription stands out. "January 1886," it notes, "Bitter cold. Thick ice lasting from Friday 7th until Thursday 14th. Oranges all frozen—ground frozen from 8th to 13th. The longest and most severe spell of cold since we came here in 1854."

*Historic Haile Homestead at Kanapaha Plantation is three miles west of I-75 (Exit 384) at 8500 SW Archer Rd. (SR 24) in Gainesville. The house museum is open 10 a.m. to 2 p.m. Saturday, noon to 4 p.m. Sunday, and by appointment; admission is $5, free for children under 12. For more, visit www.hailehomestead.org or call (352) 336-9096.*

# Matheson House

*Gainesville*

Today it is one of the most interesting nineteenth-century residences in the Gainesville area, but the Matheson House began its existence in 1857 as a modest farmhouse built by a settler from Camden, South Carolina. Alexander Matheson chose Sweetwater Branch, at the eastern edge of the new town of Gainesville to start his life in Florida, but moved his family back home to South Carolina when the Civil War erupted.

It was Alexander's brother, James Douglas Matheson, who returned to the Florida community that had been incorporated only in 1854, to build the home that is now ranked as Gainesville's second-oldest residence. James had served in the Seventh South Carolina Cavalry, under Robert E. Lee, and brought his bride, Augusta Florida Steele, to live in the growing town—and in a house that would soon grow too.

Born and raised in Cedar Key, the daughter of a judge, Augusta may have met the young Confederate veteran while she was visiting the relatively large new town of Gainesville—perhaps after traveling there on the new Florida Railroad, as many others did during that expansive period. Augusta and James married and settled into the frame house that sits on a small rise facing downtown Gainesville; while his wife managed the home and the four children that came along, James became a successful dry-goods merchant.

Out-of-town relatives arrived often on the train, which ran eight blocks south of their home, and "Gussie" occasionally accompanied her husband to New York to marvel at the tall buildings and busy streets, and to buy merchandise for his store, which was across the street from the then-new Alachua County Courthouse. Back home in Gainesville, she recorded in her diary, the couple would be dining on fresh oysters that had been sent by express train from Cedar Key.

Comfortable, if not cosmopolitan, the Matheson home grew along with the family and its prominence. James developed his commercial interests but also became active in politics and cultural affairs. He served as county commissioner between1895 and 1899, in 1909 became county treasurer and was a trustee of East Florida Seminary.

By 1907, the house had grown in size and importance too. The back porch had been partly enclosed, there were bedrooms on the second story and a ground-floor sitting room, as well as gabled dormers and a gambrel roof that lent a pleasing eclecticism to the home's original blend of two styles: South Carolina plantation and Classical Revival raised cottage.

Today, its broad front porch offers deep

shelter for the home's tall windows, with its ceiling-to-ground columns, and such decorative updates as the Gothic Revival finial at the peak of the stick-style dormer centered over the wide front door add further interest to its core vernacular. A rectangular transom over the front door allows light to shine into the hallway, as do sidelights flanking the door. Period furnishings like the ornate 1840s-era bed in the front bedroom, along with personal items from the family, create a vivid impression of nineteenth-century life in a prosperous central Florida town.

The couple's son, Christopher, studied at East Florida Seminary and The Citadel, and lived in the family home while serving as the city's mayor from 1910 to 1917. He went on to the Florida Legislature in 1917, but left his law practice to serve the ministry in Oklahoma for the next twenty-six years; he returned home to Gainesville in 1946 with his wife, Sarah. She deeded Matheson House, which had been listed on the National Register of Historic Places in 1973, to the Alachua County Historic Trust upon her death in 1996.

*Matheson House is part of the Matheson Museum Inc., 513 E. University Ave., Gainesville, and is open by appointment only. For fees and more information, visit www.mathesonmuseum. org or call (352) 378-2280.*

# Herlong Mansion

*Micanopy*

The center section of the massive, three-story Herlong mansion in Micanopy was built in 1845 by R. S. Simonton. His granddaughter, Natalie Simonton, later married V. C. Herlong, a lumberman and citrus grower who had come to Micanopy from South Carolina.

The early house had a kitchen connected to the main wing by a breezeway. Around 1910, Herlong transformed the simple house into an imposing mansion. He added front rooms and another story, incorporating the kitchen and encasing the old frame structure in a brick shell built in a pleasant Classic Revival imitation of the Southern plantation design.

The interior, finished in the Arts and Crafts style of the early twentieth century, boasts architectural ornamentation that showcases the hardwood of his trade. The exterior of the twenty-room house is gracious. Its two-story veranda on the façade is supported by enormous Corinthian columns. On the second-level porch, the huge, ornate capitals of the carved-wood columns barely rise above the trim railings. The view from the veranda is of a garden shaded by oak and pecan trees, a brick front walk to the street, and a low brick and stone wall fence separating the land from historic Cholokka Boulevard, the town's main street.

In 1987, while restoring the mansion, Kim and Simone Evans, former owners of the bed-and-breakfast hotel, stripped away layers of wax and varnish from inlaid floors, paneling, and trim. They discovered that seven kinds of wood—including maple, walnut, cedar, cypress, and mahogany—had been used in the construction and remodeling. About ninety percent of the interior is now tiger oak. The original portion was made of pine. Two of the guest bedrooms, with their fireplaces and pine floors, and two downstairs fireplaces remain from the original house.

Since then, Carolyn and Stephen West have refurbished the mansion with antiques they brought from Key West. The third floor of the mansion, which used to be a ballroom, now has four additional bedrooms and suites. The old pump house and carriage house on the property have also been renovated into guest cottages.

Micanopy, a town known for its historic buildings and antique shops, is a thirty-minute drive from Silver Springs, Ocala, and the horse farms. It is fifteen minutes from Gainesville and the University of Florida, and about fifteen minutes from Marjorie Kinnan Rawlings's house at Cross Creek.

*Room rates vary at the Herlong Mansion, located on Cholokka Boulevard in Micanopy. For further information, call (352) 466-3322 or 1-800-HERLONG, or visit www.herlong.com.*

# Rawlings House

## Cross Creek

The Rawlings House, a simple Cracker structure, was the full-time home of author Marjorie Kinnan Rawlings from 1928 until 1941. There, often sitting on her porch, at a large table with a base made from a cabbage palm log, she wrote *Cross Creek,* the Pulitzer Prize–winning novel *The Yearling,* and other novels and short stories.

When Rawlings bought the house and seventy-four acres in 1928 and moved to Florida from the Northeast, it was to devote herself to writing Gothic romances. But her approach changed, with the encouragement of her editor Maxwell Perkins at Scribners. Her writing became based on her backwoods neighbors, local flora and fauna, and her life as a hard-working orange grove owner.

The frame house was built around 1890 with a raised floor and a pitched sheet-metal roof, which Rawlings replaced with cypress shakes. Its vernacular style is well adapted to central Florida's climate. Typical of countless Cracker houses that once dotted the state, it has open porches that admit breezes in the hot summers and offer shelter from the sun and frequent rainstorms. The many windows in the Rawlings House permit cross-ventilation. The original location of its kitchen (away from the main living and sleeping areas) assured that the heat of the wood-fired kitchen range remained at a distance. The separation of the living and cooking areas not only was practical in a hot climate, but also made sense in a flammable structure.

Even though the Rawlings House was well designed for a subtropical climate, it had to be heated during central Florida's occasional cold spells. The author kept warm during the sharp chills by building fires in fireplaces and small stoves, but she also was known to climb into her bed and write by lantern light. As her writing sold, Rawlings made improvements on her house, among them an indoor bathroom in 1933 and electricity in 1944. She covered her lamps' bulbs with upturned wooden bowls to create soft, warm, indirect light.

Rawlings's house is furnished comfortably, with several deerhide chairs and the cabbage-palm pedestal table. Her hand-carved pine bed once belonged to noted nineteenth-century Florida historian George Fairbanks. To recreate the period when Rawlings lived in the house—when the Floridians around her were neither wealthy snowbirds nor speculators, but people making a bare-bones living even before the Depression—an outhouse like hers was brought to the site. And to create a sense of how the house looked during Rawlings's long stay, an old typewriter with paper rolled in the carriage waits on the porch.

*The Marjorie Kinnan Rawlings house in Cross Creek, twenty-one miles south of Gainesville, is open daily from 9 a.m. to 5 p.m. Thursday through Monday. Admission is charged. For further information, call (352) 466-3672.*

# The Casements
## Ormond Beach

This sprawling Ormond Beach mansion is known as "the Rockefeller House," but it was built by the Rev. Harwood Huntington, an Episcopal minister.

The three-story, eighty-room home was constructed in the early 1900s in a pleasant shingled style that was popular at the time. It was designed so that most of its casement windows overlooked either the Halifax River or the Atlantic Ocean.

In 1918, however, the Huntingtons tired of Florida and moved to California. They sold their rambling mansion to Standard Oil founder John D. Rockefeller, who was ailing and had chosen Ormond Beach as a place to live. The oil magnate considered this place the healthiest spot on earth. He had wintered earlier at the nearby Hotel Ormond and found the climate so fine that he bought the Huntington house and set about making improvements.

Rockefeller had the rooms extended, the wide galleries enclosed, and a handsome wrought-iron fence built. He brought his son and three daughters to The Casements and used it as his winter home until he died there in 1937 at age ninety-eight.

In 1941, the historic property became a women's junior college, and a concrete-block dormitory was added. A decade later, it became a retirement center. In the 1960s, the house was slated for demolition to make way for a condominium. In the early 1970s,

however, the decaying, vandalized house was listed on the National Register of Historic Places and bought by the city of Ormond Beach, which converted it to a community center that offers classes and art exhibits.

Its present austere condition hardly reflects the house's earlier grandeur. When it belonged to Rockefeller, the house featured an octagonal living room and a three-story entrance decorated with a Louis Comfort Tiffany stained-glass skylight. Velvet draperies hung in the casement windows and gardens of sea grapes, laurel hedges, hibiscus, oleander, and roses swept from the house to water's edge. Goldfish swam in pools in the gardens, where paths were arranged in geometric patterns that followed the hedges and criss-crossed beds of flowers.

*The Casements, at 25 Riverside Drive in Ormond Beach, is open from 9 a.m. to 9 p.m. Monday through Thursday, 9 a.m. to 5 p.m. Friday, and 9 a.m. to noon on Saturday. Free tours are conducted 10 a.m. to 3 p.m. Monday through Friday, 10 a.m. to noon Saturday. For further information, call (904) 676-3216.*

# DeBary Hall

## DeBary

⚜

Even though it sits today on a ten-acre site, a calm and graciously landscaped area surrounded by suburbia, DeBary Hall still exudes the air of mystery, elegance, and history that characterized it during its heyday, when it crowned a four-hundred-acre estate, complete with its own spring-fed pool and icehouse. The manor stands high above the St. Johns River today, as obviously a mansion dedicated to entertainment and luxury now as it was when its Italianate "wedding-cake" design was completed in 1871.

The two-story, eight-thousand-square-foot frame structure began life as a hunting estate for Samuel Frederick DeBary, a German-born wine merchant of Belgian heritage whose local parties became famous for their abundant champagne. He had been wintering at the Brock House in Enterprise, Florida, in 1970; when he decided to build his own home in the area, he acquired three parcels of land from Oliver and Amanda Arnett, earlier settlers whose first home still stands on the property. The couple had acquired the land just five years earlier, from Elijah Watson of Enterprise, at the dawn of the Steamship Era.

But DeBary Hall was from the start very different from the simple Arnett House, a six-hundred-square-foot building that shows its humble background in both style and workmanship. The interior walls

of the smaller structure, described on an 1882 survey of the Debary estate as merely "tenant's quarters," are unplastered horizontal boards, with black-painted baseboards. Its floors are wide pine planks and its hand-hewed foundations rest on hand-packed brick piers.

The slightly newer twenty-room DeBary Hall, in sharp contrast, graced its grounds while showing vernacular aspects in the verandahs that enclose its two stories, as well as by its fashionable architectural style and lavish amenities. These amenities include fireplaces in each of its seven bedrooms, running water, hand-carved cornices, blown-glass panes in floor-to-ceiling windows, and the region's first swimming pool, fed by springs. That first year, DeBary made annual sojourns from his New York home to spend winters in warmth and comfort, entertaining northern guests who arrived by steamboat and often stayed for weeks or months. According to legend, DeBary counted Ulysses S. Grant and Grover Cleveland among his notable guests.

Naturally, given DeBary's prominence as an importer of Mumm's and other fine French wines, his parties were legendary; activities at DeBary Hall, however, centered more on sport hunting, swimming, and fishing. By the early 1880s, thanks largely to DeBary's new steamship service on the St. Johns, tourism

was booming and he was able to export the citrus and pecans he had begun to grow on the estate, which by then had been greatly expanded by the purchase of an additional nine thousand acres.

DeBary died in 1898, but his heirs continued wintering at DeBary Hall until 1941, when his great-granddaughter died in an airplane crash. The Hall was added to the National Register of Historic Places on July 24, 1972. Today's visitor can tour the airy, light-filled mansion, with its fine restoration and grand furnishings, along with the estate's restored 120-year-old stable and other historic outbuildings.

*DeBary Hall Historic Site, located at 210 Sunrise Blvd. in DeBary, is open 10 a.m. to 4 p.m. Thursday through Saturday, noon to 4 p.m. Sunday. For fees and more information, visit www. debaryhall.com or call or (386) 736-5953.*

# Bradlee-McIntyre House

## Longwood

This turreted Victorian mansion, the last of the elegant winter "cottages" once common in the Altamonte Springs area, was built in 1885 for the Nathan Bradlee family of Boston.

When it was new, the house stood on what is now the busy intersection of Maitland Avenue and State Road 436 in Altamonte Springs. (It was moved in the early 1970s.) But when it was new, the large fifteen-room Queen Anne–style home was in the country, far from an Orlando that then had sandy roads and a small population. At that time, Altamonte Springs and the areas around it were resort centers for Northerners drawn by central Florida's mild winters. Many of them stayed at the famous Altamonte Springs Hotel.

Over the years, the rambling three-story frame house acquired an unlikely legend. Although U.S. President and Civil War general Ulysses S. Grant died the year it was built, a persistent rumor had it that he visited or slept in this house. The truth is that after the general's death, his son and/or his wife spent time vacationing at the house.

It changed hands several times between 1899 and 1904, when the mansion became the property of S. Maxwell McIntyre. Earlier, he had bought most of the town of Altamonte Springs from the Altamonte Land, Hotel & Navigation Co. The McIntyres occupied the house until 1946. By the 1970s, the mansion had fallen on hard times and was threatened with demolition. Deserted and vandalized, it was placed on the National Register of Historic Places and moved to Longwood by the Central Florida Society for Historic Preservation.

It has been substantially restored to its earlier grandeur, both inside and out. Among its notable features are the octagonal turret that is clad with a decorative pattern made of shingles of varying shapes, the ornate "gingerbread" woodwork that ornaments the deep gables, and the broad, first-story veranda.

The house has been furnished in styles of the late Victorian period. Living room furnishings include a turn-of-the-century Steinway piano, a rosewood Empire sofa and matching gooseneck rocker, a small Victorian love seat, and a large pier mirror. The living room and dining room are papered in soft green-and-white patterned paper. Bedroom furnishings include a carved Victorian bed and a Jenny Lind spool bed that were in the house when the McIntyres lived there.

*The Bradlee-McIntyre House is at 150 W. Warren Street in Longwood. Hours are 11 a.m. to 4 p.m., second and fourth Wednesdays and 1 p.m. to 4 p.m., second and fourth Sundays. A $1.00 donation is charged. For further information, call (407) 332-0225.*

# The Captain and The Cowboy

*Apopka*

Now a restaurant, but once a residence, this Apopka house continues to evoke an earlier Florida. The turreted house was built in 1903 by the Eldredge family, whose descendants still live in the central Florida community. In the 1920s, the eight-room frame structure became the home and clinic of Dr. T. E. McBride, one of Apopka's first physicians. After his death in 1978, it sat empty for several years. Finally, in 1985, the four-thousand-square-foot Queen Anne house was divided into four sections and moved to its present site off U.S. Highway 441 at Martin's Pond. It was enlarged and transformed into a restaurant with a Victorian atmosphere. Its latest owners removed the termite-damaged kitchen and a bathroom and added about ten thousand square feet to the elegant building while retaining its highly ornamental character. There is now dining in all rooms of the three-story house.

The high-ceilinged rooms are furnished with antiques and papered with Victorian-style patterns that are in keeping with its period of ornate design. Every room has a different theme: one is done as a children's rumpus room, complete with antique toys and paintings of children; another is a game room that features a deep-brown-and-black color scheme, thick brocades on chair seats, and old golf clubs and hunting trophies. Two of the rooms have been dedicated to the McBrides, and among the objects displayed in the rooms are 1940s vintage photographs of Mrs. McBride in some of the airplanes she flew.

The restaurant's owners spent about a year collecting period furnishings. Many of its oak tables and chairs came from the old Ormond Beach Hotel, long a coastal landmark. The carpet in the main dining room has a Victorian pattern and adds to the overall re-creation of the nineteenth century in Florida.

The house features floors and woodwork in Florida heart pine, as well as doors, casings, and a staircase in their elaborate, original state. The fireplace tiles are in greens and aquamarines. A broad porch wraps around the façade on the first floor, raised above ground level; dormers and picturesque chimneys project from the steep roof in a complex jumble of asymmetrical massing that is typical of the Queen Anne style. Today, the greatly expanded old Eldredge-McBride House is painted a crisp white with dark green trim and sits comfortably on an open site in Apopka.

*The Captain and The Cowboy is at 604 E. Main Street in Apopka, at the intersection of U.S. Highway 441 and State Road 436. High tea is served from 3 p.m. to 4 p.m. Monday through Saturday, and dinner from 5 p.m. to 11 p.m. Monday through Saturday. For further information, call (407) 886-7100.*

# Leu House

*Orlando*

When the first section of the Leu House was built sometime between 1888 and 1901, the farmhouse stood in the country. The house consisted of two rooms downstairs, with one large room featuring a fireplace and a smaller room believed to be the parlor. The upstairs had three bedrooms. Over the years, the three subsequent owners added rooms to the once-simple farmhouse, transforming it into a stately Southern home with ten distinct rooms.

The trim house, now not far from booming downtown Orlando, stands in a fifty-acre botanical garden near the largest formal rose garden in Florida and among one of the largest camellia collections in the United States. This land is what remains of the large parcel of land claimed on the shores of Lake Rowena by Angeline May Mizell while her husband was fighting for the Confederacy during the Civil War.

The first structure on the site was the family's log cabin, which stood near the present house. The nearby Mizell family graveyard is still visited by family and visitors. In the early years of the century, the Leu House was owned by wealthy New Yorker Duncan Pell who came to Florida to plant citrus, play polo, and marry silent-screen actress Helen Louise Gardner. The house gained two wings, one of which was turned into a dining room, and two porches that offered cooling shade from the summer heat. An outdoor kitchen was built a short distance from the house, which spared the main house from the cooking heat and threat of fire.

Between 1906 and 1928, it was the home of a wealthy Birmingham industrialist, Joseph Woodward, who wintered there with his family and staff. More additions were added, with plenty of renovations to the house. In 1936, it became the property of Harry P. Leu, a prosperous businessman and Orlando native who loved to travel and collect plants from around the world to place in his garden. He and his wife transformed the estate into a botanical paradise and in 1961 donated their estate to the city of Orlando.

The restored interior of the house features the sort of period furnishings and decor a successful citrus grower might have had between the 1870s and the early 1900s. Pieces on display include an ornate carved bed, Gov. Napoleon Bonaparte Broward's mahogany library table, and a round oak table and server from the Joseph A. Bumby home in Orlando.

*The Leu House Museum, 1920 N. Forest Avenue in Orlando, is open from 10 a.m. to 4 p.m. It is closed for the month of July and on December 25. Tours of the house are conducted every half hour. Admission to the Leu House Museum is included in the garden admission. For further information, call (407) 246-2620 or visit www.leugardens.org.*

# E. P. Porcher House

*Cocoa*

The elegant coquina-stone house in Cocoa was built around 1915 for citrus grower E. P. Porcher and his wife Byrnina Peck. The house is on the National Register of Historic Places, and the stone used to build it was quarried locally.

Porcher, co-founder of the Florida Citrus Commission and an innovator, believed that the fruit he grew in his Deerfield Citrus Groves would bring a higher price at market if it were washed, stamped, and attractively packaged. So he invented the first fruit-washing machine, a dolly for lifting packed fruit for storage and shipment, and the fruit stamp for labeling his produce.

Several historical styles are combined in this house that citrus built, a symmetrical, three-story stone structure. The two-story, semicircular porch at the entrance is reminiscent of a Renaissance or classical temple, and the pediment of the dormer directly over the entrance porch evokes images of Greek architecture. The house itself is more than five thousand square feet in size and is designed in a pleasant Federal style. Mrs. Porcher's interest in bridge shows in the club-, spade-, diamond-, and heart-shaped designs carved in the coquina stone on the house's back porch.

Inside, the house is impressive. A central staircase with squared spindles on its balustrade leads from the first floor to the second. There are five rooms on the first floor, along with a foyer, gallery, and kitchen. The downstairs ceilings are fourteen feet high. There are nine rooms on the second floor, where ceilings are twelve feet high. When the house was used by the Porcher family, the third floor contained bedrooms.

When the coquina-stone mansion on the Indian River was new, a warehouse and packing plant stood nearby. The packing-and-storage house was known in Cocoa as the "fruit laundry." Later, it was torn down to allow for widening of the riverfront property. The house is currently unfurnished.

*The E. P. Porcher House, located at 434 Delannoy Avenue in Cocoa, is open 8 a.m. to 5 p.m. weekdays, 10 a.m. to 2 p.m. Saturday, and by appointment. For further information, call (321) 639-3500.*

# Gamble Place

## Port Orange

Egwanulti, the bungalow James Gamble built as his country house on Spruce Creek early in the century, is only a small part of Gamble Place, a remarkable complex of historic structures west of Port Orange in Volusia County. But with its environmentally sensitive design and quaint name—from the Indian term for "by the water"—the Cracker-style house sets the tone for the cluster of buildings around it and the 150-acre Spruce Creek Environmental Preserve on which it rests.

The complex includes the citrus-packing barn built in the same year by the proprietor of Proctor & Gamble, who, since his honeymoon in 1862, regularly left his native Ohio to winter in Daytona Beach, most of the time in his Queen Anne mansion on Silver Beach, Koweeka ("here we rest"). In 1983, the soap magnate's rustic retreat was given to the Nature Conservancy by his heirs.

Also at Gamble Place are a gazebo built by local craftsmen who used lumber from the property, hundreds of century-old azaleas in Gamble's flowering gardens, and Gamble Landings, his dock on the upper reaches of meandering Spruce Creek. Though the Gamble family and friends often traveled to Egwanulti by horse and buggy, picnic hampers on board, they also reached it via the Landings in their open-air yacht, *Seabreeze*.

One of the most intriguing aspects of the complex is a playhouse built in 1938 near Gamble House by Gamble's son-in-law and named Wee Ki Wah ("clear water"). Judge Alfred K. Nippert modeled the Snow White House after the 1937 Walt Disney classic film; he used twenty original animated cells to create the "black forest" house with cypress from the property, and there played host to Disney himself that same year, long before Disney's theme parks came into being. The Snow White House isn't far from another, equally fantastic structure: a "Witch's Hut" made from the hollow trunk of a huge cypress.

However, it is Egwanulti that most enchants. The house was built on land Gamble bought on April 16, 1898, complete with citrus groves planted after the great freeze of 1895 for $600 from George Leffman. He, in turn, had purchased the tract not long before from his brother Robert Leffman, who had acquired it in 1886 through a United States land grant authorized by President Chester A. Arthur. The tract's verdant longleaf-pine forests, steep banks at Leffman Branch (or Gamble Slough), and rolling sandhills testify to its primeval heritage.

The updated "Cracker" residence, built in memory of his wife Margaret, who died in 1901, testifies to Gamble's interests in Florida vernacular architecture and his yearning for a tranquil, "Thoreau-esque"

glade. The unpretentious house, where Gamble played host to such luminaries as President William Howard Taft, H. J. Heinz, and John D. Rockefeller, his neighbor from The Casements in nearby Ormond Beach, incorporates such features as the large windows, porches for informal late-night chair-rocking gatherings, a lengthy dogtrot that separates the kitchen from the rest of the house, and whimsical touches such as the crescent moon designs on its shutters—familiar Southern motifs, reinterpreted here.

The house was rarely used by Gamble as a chief residence. Visits to the rustic retreat were usually for just a day and evening during the winter months, with the party hunting and fishing during the daylight hours, picnicking, and playing cards after sunset before returning to their homes in the Daytona Beach area. Indeed, during the early 1900s, only the caretaker who is said to haunt the grounds was a permanent resident. After Gamble's death in 1932, the property passed to his daughters, whose heirs donated the environmentally sensitive site and historic buildings to the Nature Conservancy.

In 1988 the Daytona Beach Museum of Arts and Sciences entered into an agreement with the Nature Conservancy and since then has managed the property. Today, the soap baron's country home stands at the heart of a pristine preserve where alligators, ospreys, and other wildlife roam freely. Its simple lines muted by a subtle cream-and-green palette, Gamble House offers visitors a special slice of Old Florida.

*Gamble Place is located at 1819 Taylor Road in Port Orange, 1.5 miles west of I-95. For more information contact the Museum of Arts and Sciences at 352 S. Nova Road, Daytona Beach, FL 32114; call (386) 255-0285 or visit www.moas.org.*

# Waterhouse Residence

## Maitland

The two-story frame house on a slope overlooking the shores of Lake Lily in old Fort Maitland in 1884 is a fine example of vernacular design and a charming blend of Northern and Southern architectural styles. Its tall, two-over-two sash windows allow breezes to cool its interior, as does circulation below its raised floor. Breezes in the Waterhouse residence enter windows on an L-shaped veranda shaded from the sun and sheltered from rain. Some original shutters survive, painted green and placed on windows over a century ago to protect against stormy weather, and this sturdy home was built with an abundant local wood: warm heart pine from Orlando that has endured in its exterior shiplap siding, wainscoting, simple window-and-door moldings, and Eastlake-style turned stair rails.

Evocative as the Waterhouse residence is, placed at the center of a town that was small but thriving when the house was built, it is much more than an outstanding, well-preserved example of frame vernacular. In 1882, just before William Henry Waterhouse moved to Maitland from his native Long Island and constructed his home, the town was newly formed, "a scattered little hamlet, comprising four or five business houses." Two years later, as the house took shape on a tree-shaded spot, Maitland had grown.

Waterhouse, a builder by trade and a veteran of the Civil War whose health had been damaged by a year-long confinement in the Confederate prison at Andersonville, Georgia, moved to Maitland as it began to develop. He purchased his piece of land on the south side of Lake Lily from Edward C. Hungerford in 1883, in the settlement by then known as Lake Maitland. He constructed many other houses in the area, and photographs and other records indicate that he was respected as a craftsman. In some documents, he is referred to as an architect, so he probably designed as well as constructed homes. He also designed the town's library; his original structure may be seen among later additions.

Besides his work as a local builder, Waterhouse was active in politics. He helped secure Maitland's first town charter in 1885, and served as alderman until his death in 1921.

Their family home underwent few changes as time passed. Around 1908, a second-story addition was built over the back living room, to the east, and by 1916 a larger kitchen had been built to the rear of the house, replacing the one that originally was in the current living room. By 1930, a screened porch on the first floor and a sleeping porch on the second story were added behind the 1908 addition. In the 1950s, a breezeway/pantry (or "cold room") of the sort that was common in Orange County homes was converted into a bathroom. And

around 1970, the former front parlor became a bedroom when the entire second story was converted into an apartment.

Changes to the structure were surprisingly few in that 1970 renovation. It was restored to its original single-family style and reflects the home and lifestyle of a prosperous builder in the late Victorian era, as it was during the early years of the Waterhouse tenure. There are no longer groves blossoming around the frame house, as there were when the family moved to Maitland and enjoyed the citrus trees that had been planted in 1872, but the landscaping around the house reflects the growth of domestic gardening in central Florida between the 1880s and about 1930.

The house was listed on the National Register of Historic Places in 1983. The Waterhouse family retained possession until 1986, when it was purchased by the city of Maitland. The fine old wooden house, lovingly maintained throughout its long life, was restored to its appearance before 1900, and in 1992 made its debut as a historic house museum with an interesting sidelight: a small board-and-batten carpentry shop devoted to contracting and building as they were practiced by Waterhouse. Among its highlights are a collection of woodworking tools, some from Waterhouse's own set.

*The Waterhouse Residence and Carpentry Shop Museums, 820 Lake Lily Drive in Maitland, are open noon to 4 p.m. Thursday through Sunday. Admission is free, and group hour-long tours with docents may be scheduled any time during the week. The house museum is run by the Maitland Historical Society. For more information, call (407) 644-2451.*

# Thurston House

## Maitland

The year the last brick went into place on the last of three corbeled chimneys at Thurston House in Maitland was a historic one for the community five miles north of Orlando. That same year, Fort Maitland was incorporated as the town of Maitland. That was 1885, and since then the gracious Queen Anne frame structure on the shores of Lake Eulalia has been home to three more families.

Its original owner, Cyrus B. Thurston, had built the house by the sparkling lake as a retreat from Minnesota, where the wealthy Northerner had businesses in farm implements and cold storage—and a place on the social register and "Who's Who" of his day. He died in 1915, and the Hirsch family of Glencoe, Illinois, bought the house, naming it Glencoe Groves after their hometown. A former neighbor remembers Hirsch's excursions in his chauffeured Cadillac

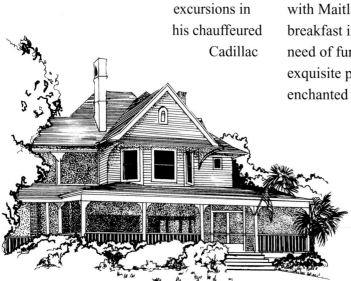

limousine, elegant down to its bud vases.

The home's next owner was Verna Goodwin, a Hirsch daughter who built herself a new home at the end of the path to Lake Catherine and sold Glencoe Groves to Mr. and Mrs. Clarence Cubbedge. For three successive terms, Mr. Cubbedge was mayor of Maitland. In 1949 the rambling house, already a Victorian prize, was sold to its last private owners, Mr. and Mrs. Arthur O'Heir. Mr. O'Heir was the owner of Maitland Plaza, a shopping mall in the heart of Maitland.

Mrs. O'Heir sold the home to the city of Maitland in 1988, and it was designated as heritage land. The house sat empty on its eight acres of woodland for two years, surrounded by fruit trees, azaleas, and flower and herb gardens. Joe and Carole Ballard discovered the house and began negotiations with Maitland to convert it into a bed-and-breakfast inn. Even in its rather sad state—in need of furnishings, with paint layered on exquisite pine and cypress paneling—it enchanted them. After six months of patient

scraping and $200,000 in renovation costs, they transformed Glencoe Groves into the stately, welcoming Thurston House.

Each of its three guest bedrooms (each with a private bath) today bears the name of a former owner, and the house has a comfortable turn-of-the-century style that fits well with the high-ceilinged, big-windowed parlors and wraparound porch. The Ballards opened their inn in September 1992. The property is leased from the city of Maitland, but the Ballards are the sole owners of the business known as Thurston House. On warm evenings, as guests sip sparkling refreshments on the veranda or gaze over the gardens during breakfast, it is easy to forget that this is the turn of another century. Surrounded by gardens and birdsong, Thurston House is an island of serenity and Old Florida charm.

*Thurston House, 851 Lake Avenue in Maitland, may be visited during regular business hours by advance arrangement. For more information on rates, reservations, and visits, call (407) 539-1911.*

# DeLand House Museum

## DeLand

When the DeLand House Museum was new, in 1886, it was a small and rather modest residence. Built for George Hamlin, DeLand's first attorney and developer of the Hamlin orange, it was a story-and-a-half structure on a large lot that stretched an entire city block to the town's main street, Woodland Boulevard. Just seven years later, however, the founder of Stetson University bought the Hamlin house and converted it into faculty housing. John B. Stetson, the hat manufacturer and local benefactor whose gifts to the university that bears his name were many and generous, also donated the still-new frame home.

Just ten years after that, a Stetson professor purchased and enlarged the house. It took on a classical appearance under Dr. Charles Farriss, a professor of Greek. Dr. Farriss raised the roof, added a second story, and moved an interior stairway. He enjoyed working with stained and leaded glass, and his work can be seen around the main entrance, over the north entrance, over the fireplace in the north parlor, and in dining room cabinets.

Dr. Farriss also provided his stately home with a number of conveniences that are reminiscent of Thomas Jefferson's Monticello. The trolley in a narrow passageway between the two parlors carries wood to both and remains hidden behind small doors beside the fireplaces when it isn't being used. Cabinets made of richly grained heart of pine can be opened from either formal parlor, or a dining room to its west; the cabinets in the dining room feature Dr. Farriss's clean-lined leaded-glass doors.

Dr. Farriss also added the gleaming pine floors, high ceilings, multiple windows, paneled kitchen, and the graceful two-story neo-classical pediment over its original entrance, toward Woodland Boulevard to the east. Among the house's most striking features is the bow-bay window in the formal south parlor; it is not known whether it was original to the house or was added by Dr. Farriss.

Between his tenure and the wartime years of the 1940s, when it was turned into apartments, the house changed hands several times and continued to expand, with the addition of pleasant sunrooms on its western façade. In 1988, Robert and Hawtense Conrad bought the house and donated it to the city of DeLand, which restored it to its former glory. Nearly all of its furnishings were gifts, and the vintage art and photographs that adorn the house's walls depict the history of West Volusia County.

Artifacts and memorabilia throughout the home, from turn-of-the-century china to the cutwork coverlet and antique dolls, evoke the graceful spirit of an early-twentieth-century college town.

The DeLand House Museum was named in honor of Henry DeLand, who in 1876 founded the city and in 1884 founded Lake Helen, the smaller town to the south of DeLand. The original house was built on land purchased from Henry DeLand, whose coat, hat, and walking stick hang from hooks in the kitchen. In DeLand House, more than in other house museums, the spirit of the past seems to linger—and to be ready to tell its stories.

*The Henry A. DeLand House Museum is at 137 W. Michigan Avenue in DeLand. Admission is $3.00 per adult. Students, children, and members of the West Volusia Historical Society are free. Hours are 12 p.m. to 4 p.m. Tuesday through Saturday. For more information, call (386) 740-6813 or visit www.delandhouse.com.*

# Mary McLeod Bethune House

*Daytona Beach*

The Mary McLeod Bethune House is a two-story wood frame building located on the campus of Bethune-Cookman University. It is an example of frame vernacular architecture. The building has an irregular plan and a gable roof with a hip extension. An end porch with a hip roof and tapered column supports extends from the façade. Other notable architectural features include a west end, exterior chimney, and a continuous brick foundation.

In 1905 the house was built for A. B. and Fannie Reddick. In December 1913, James Gamble, of Proctor and Gamble Company, and Thomas White, president of White Sewing Machine Company, bought the house for Mrs. Bethune. It served as her residence until her death. On March 17, 1953, with Mrs. Roosevelt as her guest speaker, she dedicated "The Retreat" to become the Mary McLeod Bethune Foundation. She wanted the foundation to preserve her papers, to support Bethune-Cookman College through scholarships, to foster interracial good will, and to inspire youth.

In the Foundation are Mrs. Bethune's original furnishings, photographs of many prominent people, including President Franklin D. Roosevelt and Walter White of the National Association for the Advancement of Colored People. The Foundation is now a National Historic Landmark as well as a United Methodist Church Historic Site.

In December 2005 the Historic Preservation Advisory Council Bureau of Historic Preservation Florida Department of State awarded the Mary McLeod Bethune Foundation a $300,000 grant to preserve the home of Dr. Mary McLeod Bethune.

*The Mary McLeod Bethune Foundation is located on the Campus of Bethune-Cookman University, 640 Dr. Mary McLeod Bethune Blvd, Daytona Beach. It is open Monday through Friday 10:00 a.m. to 4:00 p.m. and Saturday 10:00 a.m. to 2:00 p.m. Admission is free. For more information call (386) 481-2122.*

# Seven Sisters Inn

## *Ocala*

The cheerful Seven Sisters bed-and-breakfast inn, colorful in its painted-lady pinks and blues, is a gracious reminder of Ocala's long history. The three-story frame structure dates from 1888, not long after many of the central Florida community's structures were lost in a devastating conflagration.

The mansion was built for the Scott family. Though it rose in the era now dubbed "brick-city days" in reference to the post-1886 desire for fireproof structures, is only partly of brick. Its two massive chimneys, like the piers on which it rests, are brick, but the house's main material is wood. That's appropriate for its location and its style, an ornate Queen Anne with an expansive porch that extends across its entire façade and wraps around each side. Its many doorways and its six mantelpieces are of heart pine and walnut, according to innkeeper Bonnie Morehardt. Its original owners lived in their frame house for about forty-five years, and then it changed hands five times. It was converted into apartments and by the 1970s it had become dilapidated.

It was approaching demolition when the latest of many owners moved in and began repairs. And by 1985, when the first and most major of its renovations ended, the picture was entirely different: the following year the Scott mansion was named "Best Restoration Project" in the state by the Florida Trust for Historic Preservation. It was owned and operated by Bonnie Morehardt and Ken Oden, who lived in the multicolored cottage behind the main house.

When they took over the inn, the seven guest rooms had been christened for its then-owner's seven sisters. Most remain, made more luxurious with the addition of private baths, big beds, and such amenities as fireplaces, designer fabrics, jacuzzis, walk-in showers, and computer hookups. One particularly large room, at about thirteen hundred square feet, is "Lottie's Loft" on the atticlike third floor. And the newest room was named in honor of someone who might be considered one brother, Ms. Morehardt's co-owner Ken. That room is as exotic as the taste for Orientalism at the fin-de-siècle, with its lacquered-red walls and Japanese antiques. The lush tropical plantings around the colorful inn, like the furnishings that mix yesterday and today, evoke the past fancifully, and very pleasantly, as a sunny retreat.

*Seven Sisters Inn, 820 SE Fort King Street, Ocala, is open throughout the year. For more information or reservations, call (352) 867-1170 or (800) 250-3496 or visit www. sevensistersinn.com.*

# Clifford House

*Eustis*

The Clifford House, at the corner of Bay and Bates Streets in Eustis, is in graceful antebellum style, complete with a deep porch that extends across its façade and around much of one side. Its low lines, broad massing, balustraded "widow's walk," and double-columned, pedimented two-story entry speak volumes of easy living in a long-ago South. Yet the eighteen-room mansion dates only from 1911, because of forces well beyond the control of its owners and, indeed, everyone involved in growing Florida citrus at the end of the last century.

Guilford David Clifford, a native of Rome, New York, who pioneered in the tractless Florida wilderness in the years soon after the end of the Civil War, actually planned his ample home in 1894, on the eve of the devastating freeze of December 1894 and the even worse back-to-back freezes of February 1895. He had come to the territory in its earliest stages and opened its first general store in the two-room house he constructed after arriving in the area then known as the Highlands.

Clifford was one of seven settlers who met in Jacksonville in the summer of 1875—and one of three who stayed in the town they founded, to became the founding fathers of Eustis. The group made a sixty-hour trip down the St. Johns River into Mellonville Landing, the site of present-day Sanford. They then set off to find land suitable for settling. They made their way to Lake Woodward, where Clifford purchased 160 acres at $1.25 an acre and applied for title to the property. He went back to Jacksonville and turned around with a new wagon loaded with his household goods and enough lumber for his first structure.

One of its rooms became the Lake Woodward Store, the first in the region, and the other became the home Clifford would share with his family. By 1876, the family had built a two-story community building, the site of town meetings and Friday night assemblies. The first school rose nearby in the winter of 1876–77, as did the homes of A. S. Pendry and other prominent new townspeople. The town's original name was Pendryville, but in 1880 its name was changed to Lake Eustis; in 1881, it was changed again, to Eustis.

By that time, the town was thriving, as were Clifford's many business interests. The 1886–87 Florida Gazetteer and Business Directory describes him as dealing in "grocery, hardware, building material, fertilizers, stoves, crockery and glassware, hay and grain" in the "live and wide-awake city." He became trustee of the first Eustis school in 1876, retaining that role for more than thirty years. Clifford also developed the Greenwood Cemetery, which he owned from 1885 until 1902, seventeen years before his death.

The two-and-a-half story home he built outside of town, on a quiet dirt road, stands as his greatest monument today. He had gone back to New York to meet with an architect for his home's plans in 1894 and was making

arrangements for construction to begin when the weather turned unusually cold. By the end of the last freeze, the state's economy had been shattered; Clifford was prosperous, but he was forced to extend credit to needy customers.

Construction finally began on the neo-classical structure in January 1910, and continued for almost two years. His granddaughter Charlotte Wilson recalled that he "never had but four men working at one time" because he liked keeping up with what each worker was doing. He built the 4,500-square-foot structure to last, of Florida cypress with double layers of three-quarter-inch Florida pine for the floors. Each of six fireplaces features imported Italian tiles in different designs and mirrored oak mantels.

Each of the seven bedrooms has both closets and armoires. Clifford disliked wasting space and incorporated many clever built-in elements. One cedar cupboard was placed at the top of the stairs on the second floor, and the dining-room breakfront served a double purpose: food could be served from it, and when it was rolled away from the wall, a Murphy bed dropped down from it.

In every way, his home was elegant, commodious, and convenient. It had indoor plumbing and large windows for maximum cross-ventilation. Walls were plaster of Paris, pristine white and never painted, and even today the house has all of its original woodwork. Its windows, hinged at the sides for easy cleaning, were copper-screened.

The home was occupied by five generations of the Clifford family, from 1912 until Clifford and Unity's descendants made it the home of the Eustis Historical Museum and Preservation Society.

*The Clifford House museum, located at 536 Bay St. in Eustis, is open 1 p.m. to 5 p.m. Tuesday and Thursday, 2 p.m. to 5 p.m. Sunday in summer and fall; 10 a.m. to 5 p.m. Monday through Saturday and 1 p.m. to 5 p.m. Sunday for Christmas in Eustis; 2 p.m. to 5 p.m. Sundays only during the summer. For appointments and more information, call (352) 483-0046.*

# IV
## Southwest Florida

Cà d'Zan, Sarasota

## Southwest Florida

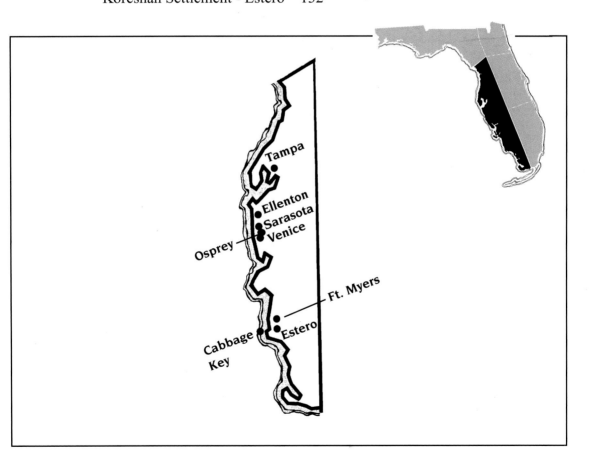

# Sun and Sand

The earliest recorded European visit to the Tampa area was in 1528, when Pánfilo de Narváez passed through it on his way north. He was exploring the interior of the New World on the first such expedition. Eleven years later, Hernando de Soto arrived and promptly conquered an Indian village in order to formally declare Spanish supremacy.

For the next three centuries, there was little development in the region the early Spanish visitors named Bahia de Espiritu Santo. In 1823, soon after Florida became a territory of the young United States, Fort Brooke was constructed of logs. Eight years later, a post office called Tampa Bay opened in the area, and, in 1834, the settlement's official name became Tampa, an Indian name meaning "split wood for quick fires." The new fort played an important role in the second of the Seminole Wars—1835 to 1842—yet Tampa itself remained a small town and the region around it virtually a wilderness.

During the Civil War, Tampa saw only minor military action. After the Confederacy fell, its population dwindled even further. And when a railroad was built between the east and west coasts, bypassing Tampa, and yellow fever swept the community, the already small population declined still further.

All that changed in 1884, when Henry Plant pushed the H. B. Plant Railroad through to Tampa, then a town of just a few hundred people. Next, he extended the road nine miles southwest to Port Tampa, where he built a causeway and piers to deep water to facilitate shipping. As in other parts of Florida where the arrival of the railroad created incredibly rapid development, Tampa seemed to change overnight.

In 1890, the year before Plant built his fabulous, Moorish-style Tampa Bay Hotel, Tampa's population was five thousand. A decade later, with the success of the cigar industry in Ybor City and the discovery of phosphate fields nearby, the population had tripled. Some thirty thousand troops were stationed in Tampa during the Spanish-American War, and Col. Theodore Roosevelt trained his Rough Riders on the grounds of the famous hotel, which is now home to the University of Tampa.

As Tampa developed into an industrial center, the nearby areas also saw rapid growth. Sarasota, to the south, had been settled in the 1840s by William Whittaker, a homesteader from Tallahassee who built a log home and planted the area's first orange grove with seeds brought from Cuba. Later, Hamilton Disston bought four million acres in the area and, in 1883, persuaded sixty Scottish families to settle on the land. Three years later, the son of a Scottish settler built a golf course in Sarasota and that, along with fishing and hunting, helped attract vacationers. A pioneer railroad ran to Sarasota in 1892, yet until 1899 the community had only twenty houses and no sidewalks.

It took the arrival of the Seaboard Air Line Railroad in 1902 to transform Sarasota. In 1911, Chicago society leader Mrs. Potter Palmer purchased a thirteen-acre estate and other property, and that same year the Ringling Brothers first came to town. Sixteen years later, John Ringling made the once-quiet town the winter home of his circus, the "greatest show on earth," and built his home, the magnificent Cà d'Zan.

The development of Fort Myers, still farther to the south, was more gradual. Settled near a fort built in 1839 and enlarged in 1850, the area was a thriving agricultural center after the Civil War. Among its crops were mangoes, avocados, papayas, guavas and citrus. Fort Myers also was known for its commercial fishing. Inventor Thomas Alva Edison built a house in the town in 1886, hoping to perfect a bamboo-filament light bulb while working in his winter laboratory and using plants that grew wild on his property. Henry Ford and Harvey Firestone, Edison's friends and sponsors, built winter homes near the inventor's in Fort Myers.

Another railroad, the short-lived Orange Belt, running from Apopka in 1883, brought life to St. Petersburg, a scruffy village barely inhabited by thirty people, including children. Peter Demens, the Americanized name of the immigrant whose dream built the railroad, named the town for his beloved Russian city. By the early 1900s, St. Petersburg was on its way to rapid growth with the arrival of people such as Charles A. Harvey and his plans to build a St. Petersburg harbor.

The stories of the main cities on Florida's west coast are very different from one another, yet all depended for their development on transportation—the train, primarily—and on tourism. As in other parts of Florida, once people came and saw, they came back and stayed.

Ford Winter Estate, Fort Myers

# Cigar Workers' Houses

## Tampa

Three frame cottages, now part of the Ybor City State Museum, are typical of those that once were common in the east Tampa community. Moved from their original sites and restored to their appearance in the heyday of cigar making, from 1895 to 1920, they are houses once occupied by cigar factory workers and their families.

The hand-rolling of cigars became an important industry in Tampa when Don Vicente Martinez Ybor opened his factory in 1886 in the sparsely populated, palmetto-covered frontier. He, like other cigar manufacturers, moved from Key West to avoid employees' demands for higher wages and better working conditions. At one time, the Ybor factory was the largest cigar-producing factory in the world and employed a fifth of Ybor City's cigar makers.

The community that sprang up around the factories included Cubans, Germans, Spaniards, Italians, and Jews. They established their own newspapers, restaurants, social clubs, mutual-aid societies, and hospitals. In addition, the residents continued the simple, practical style of residential architecture that had characterized the Key West cigar makers' houses.

The houses were built on a long, narrow, Spanish-style floor plan that has rooms lined one behind the other opening off a long hallway along one side. Often referred to as conones—cannons, or shotgun houses—it was said that a shotgun could be fired from the front door to the back without hitting a wall. Two cottages display exhibits of Ybor City's cigar-making history, but one restored cottage serves as a house museum and is furnished in a simple style typical of the period and social class.

The single-story cigar workers' houses were built in a balloon type of construction from Florida pine, with hand-split cedar or cypress shakes and pine-plank floors. They had no heat, electricity, or running water, and protection from storms and insects was provided by inside shutters and, in the hot seasons, by cheesecloth screening. The earliest houses had cypress or cedar shingles, but after the 1908 fire that destroyed whole blocks of Ybor City, roofs were covered with tin.

*The Cigar Workers' Houses are at the Ybor City State Museum, 1818 9th Avenue in Tampa. They are open from 9 a.m. to 5 p.m. Tuesdays through Saturdays. Tours are conducted at 10:30 a.m. Admission is charged. For further information, call (813) 247-6323.*

# Banyan House
*Venice*

This Mediterranean-style house—now a bed-and-breakfast inn—was built in 1926 for Robert Marvin and his wife during the height of Florida's great land boom. Marvin was an executive with the Brotherhood of Locomotive Engineers, the developers of the planned city of Venice, Florida. When the land boom bottomed out in 1929, the city went bankrupt and became a ghost town. The house, like the rest of the city, was abandoned.

The cream-colored house, with its red barrel tiles and latticed front door, was designed for luxurious living. It had ten rooms, pecky cypress ceilings, and a carriage house. But for several years—until Virginia Wilson bought it for back taxes—its inhabitants were hobos. They would camp out on the Italian tiled floors and cook over an open fire in a sculptured fireplace that also had been imported from Italy. During

Wilson's ownership, from 1932 to 1962, the house was a nursery school, a guest house, and a tearoom, as well as the offices of the city's first taxi service. During the Second World War, the Banyan House became an unofficial headquarters for the USO.

The next owner, Margaret Thomas, wrote books about sharks' teeth and displayed her fossils in the house. It is said that as she worked on her books she tossed some of her sharks' teeth rejects into the pool, which caved in while she lived at the Banyan House. The house got its name in the 1930s, when it was a rooming house, from the gigantic East India tree on the property.

The elegant house was used as a hurricane shelter during the 1930s and 1940s. In 1979, it was converted into a bed-and-breakfast inn and has been renovated to reflect the city's unusual history and the period when the house was new. The guest

rooms in the main house and the carriage house have such names as Palm Room and Palmetto Room, and the swimming pool and hot tub are set in the garden beneath the old banyan tree.

*The Banyan House is at 519 S. Harbor Drive in Venice. Rates at the bed-and-breakfast inn vary seasonally. For further information, call (941) 484-1385.*

# Gamble Plantation

## Ellenton

The Gamble Plantation in Ellenton is the only antebellum mansion on Florida's west coast that is still standing. It has survived Indian uprisings, Civil War incursions, and natural disasters. The home also is of historic interest because it served, in May 1865, as the hiding place for Judah P. Benjamin, the only Confederate cabinet member to elude capture as the South was falling to the North.

The elegant residence, begun in 1843 and completed in 1850, was built by Maj. Robert Gamble. He was a veteran of the Seminole Wars who had moved from Tallahassee in 1842 to establish an immense sugar cane plantation.

The Greek Revival structure has walls that are two feet thick for insulation. They are made of tabby bricks—tabby is a primitive form of concrete that here is a mixture of lime, crushed oyster shells, and perhaps sugarcane juice—then plastered with more tabby.

The residence is forty-three feet wide and ninety-three feet long, and its eighteen twenty-five-foot-high columns were, at the time of its construction, considered symbols of sophistication. They are made of wedge-shaped tabby bricks and are nearly eighteen inches in diameter. The columns support verandas on three sides and both levels, in typical Southern mansion style. Those large porches provide a place to sit, and open the home to cool breezes while sheltering it from sunshine and showers.

The mansion's original grounds were vast: Gamble owned a 3,500-acre site, 1,500 of which were cleared and cultivated. In 1855, he had 151 slaves working on the plantation. Today, the restored Gamble mansion looks much as it did when it was new. Inside, it has period furnishings that evoke the spirit of the vanished era. A small sugarcane field on its grounds represents the hundreds of acres once farmed.

*The Gamble Plantation, located at 3708 Patten Avenue, off U.S. Highway 301 in Ellenton, is open from 8 a.m. to 11:45 a.m. and 12:45 p.m. to 4:30 p.m. daily Thursday through Monday. Tours are offered six times daily. Admission is charged for those over age six. For further information, call (941) 723-4536.*

# Cà d'Zan

*Sarasota*

The residence of John and Mable Ringling in Sarasota is one of Florida's grandest houses. Completed in 1926 at a cost of about $1.5 million, the structure combined architectural elements drawn from several of Mrs. Ringling's favorite places—the façade of the Doge's Palace, the Ca'd'Oro on the Grand Canal in Venice, and the tower of the old Madison Square Garden in New York, where her husband's circus regularly appeared.

Designed by New York architect Dwight James Baum, the home is made of terracotta T brick and cement. The exterior is decorated in stucco with glazed tiles in a variety of colors—soft red, yellow, blue, green, and ivory. The roof of the two-and-a-half-story structure is covered with thousands of barrel tiles that were originally purchased in Granada, Spain, by Mrs. Ringling, who was involved in the design and construction of the house and gardens.

The mansion's windows are set with handmade tinted Lac glass made in France. Such elements as antique columns, doorways, and historic rooms were purchased at auctions and installed under Mable's direction. The look that the Ringlings and their designer sought was a fanciful Venetian

Gothic style, and their efforts extended to the house's interior. The house is centered by a vast court that served as the main living room, around which forty-one bedrooms and fifteen baths are located. Service areas such as kitchens and pantries, as well as servants' quarters, are in a wing to the south.

Many of the furnishings at Cà d'Zan—which in a Venetian dialect means "house of John"—were acquired from the homes of Vincent Astor and George Jay Gould. In keeping with Cà d'Zan's eclecticism, the furnishings show the influence of such varied styles as the Italian and French Renaissance and French baroque. Among the noteworthy furnishings are the Aeolian organ with its 2,289 pipes, the Steinway grand piano in its ornamented rosewood case, and the many

seventeenth-century Flemish tapestries. To add to the house's appeal, the ceilings of its ballroom and game room were painted by Willy Pogany, set designer for the Ziegfeld Follies. The game room features a portrait of the Ringlings in fancy-dress costume at Carnival in Venice.

*Cà d'Zan, on Sarasota Bay, is open from 10 a.m. to 5:30 p.m seven days a week as part of The Ringling Museum complex located at U.S. 41 and University Blvd. Closed Thanksgiving, Christmas, and New Year's Day. Admission is charged. For further information, call (941) 359-5700.*

The history of the two-story frame house at Spanish Point in Sarasota County might seem to begin a couple of years after the Civil War ended, when John Greene Webb and his young family sailed into Little Sarasota Bay and named it Spanish Point, after a Spaniard who had recommended the site during their stop in Key West.

But long before the Webbs fled the harsh winters of their native Utica, New York, and made the voyage around Key West, the high point of land projecting into the bay had been a thriving community. Part of the site's attraction—both to modern visitors and to its earlier settlers—came from the topographical results of the archaeological record that was created by those native settlers, who gradually built up tall shell middens, or scrap piles, between about 3000 B.C. and 1000 A.D.

An ancient burial mound, two middens, and an exhibit called A Window to the Past, which was created inside a midden, offer insights into the lives of early Floridians who fished, hunted, made tools from shell and bone, mended fishing nets, cooked food, and practiced funerary rites there. Other historic aspects of Spanish Point are the packing house built by Webb and his sons to prepare the crops they grew on their ten-acre farm for shipment to Cedar Key and Key West; Frank Guptill's late-nineteenth-century boat yard; the boom-era Osprey School (now the site's Visitors Center); White Cottage, built in 1884 as a dormitory for guests at Webb's Winter Resort; and Mary's Chapel, a

reconstruction of the 1894 structure built in memory of Mary Sherrill, a young musician who died of consumption while staying at the resort in the winter of 1892.

Despite all these attractions, it's the house built by Frank and Lizzie Webb Guptill on a bayfront midden in 1901, twenty-two years after they married, that speaks most eloquently of pioneer life on Florida's southeast coast. It was constructed meticulously, with such clever nautical references as fish-scale shingles, a curving banister, and a second-story bayfront porch that resembles a ship's bow. Those references were appropriate—Lizzie, one of John and Eliza Webb's five children, met and married Frank after her brothers Will and Jack met him in Cedar Key and recognized his boat-building skills.

At his new boatyard, Frank and the Webbs built a barge, sloops, and schooners, and began exporting crops, starting with sugar cane, soon after John and Eliza settled at Spanish Point. By 1878 the crops had grown to include a citrus grove of three hundred orange trees and fifty lemon and lime trees. By 1880, when the Webbs expanded their activities to bed-and-board for winter tourists, mostly in White Cottage, the Guptills were able to offer the seasonal guests Gulf cruises; indeed, a replica of the 1900 sailboat-turned-motor launch is usually moored at the Packing House dock.

The house was constructed with the climate of Spanish Point in mind, with

front and back porches that sheltered large windows. The master bedroom and living room were on the ground floor, and the stairway led from the living room to a hallway between two second-floor bedrooms. The living room's rear door opened onto the porch, which in turn led to the detached kitchen that included a dining table and small rear rooms to house the family when they made the main house's bedrooms available to boarders. According to family stories, life in the kitchen was hot enough that Lizzie was inspired to measure it—and to find that the temperature inside was 102 degrees Fahrenheit.

Other family legends include those about the pine detailing in the main house. In the living room, walls were paneled with alternating strips of light and dark pine so that firelight flickering over it in winter would produce a decorative effect. According to Rose Griffith Bryan, her uncle Frank hunted "all over the country" for a yellow-toned pine, and created a fireplace mantel and stair banister in curves of hard, oiled pine. Another special touch is the pair of double doors that open from the upstairs hallway onto the balcony. The home was the setting for more than respite from the cold, or for family life, however; Frank was a fiddler and Lizzie played the piano, and the front porch of their home was the scene of the Little Sarasota Bay community's picnic suppers, where the couple provided the area's young people with home-grown entertainment, Old Florida style.

*Guptill House at Historic Spanish Point, located at 337 North Tamiami Trail in Osprey, is on Little Sarasota Bay in Sarasota County. It is open 9 a.m. to 5 p.m. Monday through Saturday, noon to 5 p.m. Sunday; for fees or tour times, visit www.historicspanishpoint.org or call (941) 966-5214.*

# Cabbage Key Inn and Restaurant
## Cabbage Key

This pleasant, one-story frame house was completed in 1938 as a winter home for Alan Rinehart, the son of American mystery writer Mary Roberts Rinehart, author of *The Circular Staircase* and other well-known damsel-in-distress suspense novels.

The reclusive author Rinehart is said to have written some of her stories at the Cabbage Key house, as well as at her own home, one of the original beach cottages on nearby Useppa Island. She was very much involved in the design and construction of her son's house.

Alan Rinehart and his wife Grace had bought Cabbage Key Island, a tiny island near Fort Myers, in 1929 for $2,500. By the time the house was built, they had spent another $125,000 for the features that may be seen today at the small resort.

The house sits thirty-eight feet above sea level on Cabbage Key. It was constructed on a shell mound built up over the centuries by the Calusa Indians, whose now-extinct civilization dates to about 3500 B.C.

The house is painted white with green trim and is surrounded by a screened porch. Inside, the small inn and restaurant are cooled not by air conditioning but by the breezes provided by Bahama fans.

The nature trail on the grounds of the inn, which today includes three guest cottages, winds through a subtropical garden of fan palms, royal poincianas, and sabal—or cabbage—palms.

The Alan and Grace Rinehart residence first opened as a hotel in 1942. Among its attractions are its unusual elevation, its Florida vernacular architectural style, and its access to fishing and boating. Also appealing is its peculiar style of papering its restaurant walls with dollar bills autographed by guests, among them musicians Neil Young and Jimmy Buffett. According to Cabbage Key legend, the practice began years ago when a pessimistic patron tacked a dollar on the wall with his name on it. That way, so the story goes, even if he lost everything, he could still come back to the pleasant island for a drink.

*Cabbage Key Inn and Restaurant, on Milemarker 60 in southwest Florida's barrier islands, may be reached only by boat. Nonboaters may be picked up by reservation on Pine Island at Pineland Marina in Pineland. For further information, call (239) 283-2278.*

# Edison Winter Estate

## Fort Myers

When inventor Thomas Alva Edison decided to build a winter home for himself and his bride, Mina Miller, on a fourteen-acre site in Fort Myers, he displayed practicality as well as innovation. His two-story frame structure on the Caloosahatchee River is typically Queen Anne in its ornamentation and expansive, rambling plan. But it is also well suited to its subtropical setting, with a broad, shady porch on the ground level, French doors, and a pergola between the family and guest houses.

Shutters on the casement windows offer protection from storms, and fireplaces were built in many rooms to provide warmth from occasional cold spells. The swimming pool was filled by an artesian well one thousand feet deep.

Like many other frame houses in Florida, the trim, New England–style structure is well adapted to its climate. But, surprisingly, it was not built here. Edison's houses—the family one and the guest residence—are among the first prefabricated buildings in the country. Edison himself designed the plans. In 1885, the houses were built in sections in Fairfield, Maine. Those sections were shipped to Fort Myers, then largely a wilderness, in four sailing ships and were assembled in 1886. Soon afterward, the couple began wintering in the house.

The estate is still furnished with the Edison's artifacts, Edison-designed electroliers, laboratory, office, and car collection.

Edison chose Fort Myers partly because he wanted to experiment with a bamboo-filament light bulb, and he used the plants that grow plentifully on the property. His laboratory, like the house and garage, has been preserved as he left it. In the lab, visitors may see the inventor's equipment for producing natural rubber. Edison's tropical botanical garden, where he planted more than a thousand varieties of plants imported from all over the world for experimental purposes, thrives on the grounds. Most noteworthy is the banyan tree: It was two inches in diameter in 1925, when Edison's friend and Fort Myers neighbor Harvey Firestone brought it to him from India. The remarkable plant now covers about an acre of ground.

*The Edison-Ford Winter Estates, located at 2350 McGregor Boulevard in Fort Myers, are open daily, 9 a.m. to 5:30 p.m. Closed Thanksgiving and Christmas days. Admission is charged. For further information, call (239) 334-7419 or visit www.efwefla.org.*

# Ford Winter Estate

## Fort Myers

The charming home that Henry Ford bought in 1916 to be near to his dear friend Thomas Edison may seem to be a mere footnote to the more extensive estate Edison built in 1885. But the 1911 two-story frame structure next door to the Edison estate is a delightful monument, as significant for its gracious, functional design as for its prominent owner—and the guests who often visited. The houses are adjacent on McGregor Boulevard in downtown Fort Myers, so close to each other that the easiest way to reach one from the other is to walk through the picket fence dividing them at the Friendship Gate.

Edison invited the Ford family to his winter estate in 1914, and in 1916 Ford decided to become a more permanent part of the tropical paradise they enjoyed. So Henry and Clara Ford purchased The Mangoes, a three-and-a-half-acre estate with the "modest" fourteen-room home they would make their own. Their vacations were simple at The Mangoes, focused on a

garden filled with fruit trees—citrus, papaya, and, of course, mangoes—and on such quiet pleasures as fishing from their dock on the Caloosahatchee River.

Entertaining was just as pleasant in the dining room decorated with the English furniture Clara favored, as well as her choice Wedgewood china, Sheffield silver, and linens. The couple's living room was intimate, with burnished heart pine floors, ceiling beams, comfortable wicker seating, and a brick fireplace. Mornings could be spent on one of several porches, touched with greenery and wicker rocking chairs and open to the mild winter sun.

The greater importance of the home becomes clear with a visit to the Edison home. Throughout both homes, the crossovers that express the creative exchanges between the groundbreaking leaders of turn-of-the-century America are abundant and exciting.

*The Edison-Ford Winter Estates, located at 2350 McGregor Boulevard in Fort Myers, are open daily. Admission is charged for those six and older. For further information, call (239) 334-3614 or visit www.efwefla.org.*

# Koreshan Settlement

*Estero*

The high-ceilinged, pitched-roofed buildings of the Koreshan Settlement, on the banks of the Estero River near Fort Myers, reflect the idealism of its builders as well as a practical approach to the west coast's subtropical climate. Constructed during the late nineteenth and early twentieth centuries, the simple frame structures served as living, dining, recreation, and working quarters for followers of Cyrus Reed Teed, a religious visionary. Teed had led his disciples from Chicago to the remote Florida wilderness, establishing a settlement that he hoped would grow into a great "New Jerusalem" under his leadership. Teed called himself "Koresh" and his religion "Koreshanity." Central to his Koreshanity is the belief that the Earth is a hollow sphere with the Universe in the center and with life existing on the inside.

Teed instituted among his followers a way of life that included celibacy as well as communal living and ownership of all property. Teed, however, died in 1908 and his community declined, nevertheless leaving evidence of a great deal of creative energy.

Besides the planetary court (home of the all-female Koreshan ruling council), the art hall, a dining hall, and separate living quarters for men and women, there was a bakery, a general store, a boat works, machine shops, and agricultural buildings. Among the enterprises that supported the community were the making and selling of baked goods, including bread made from their special recipe. The gardens included such tropical plants as agaves, bromeliads, royal palms, sausage trees, avocados, mangoes, and sapotes.

Of the original buildings, only eleven remain. The oldest building, Damkohler Cottage, was built in 1882. The art hall and planetary court were built around 1905. The art hall, used then for band concerts, plays, and church services, is a single-story structure of Florida pine with a cypress shake shingle roof and a porch that wraps around the building.

The planetary court, also constructed of pine with cypress

shingle roof, consists of two stories with porches on both levels, four bedrooms upstairs, and three bedrooms and a meeting room downstairs.

Furnishings in the two buildings, all brought from the North by the Koreshans, are of the late nineteenth-century Victorian style. Visitors find the furnishings surprisingly elegant considering the then-remote Florida frontier location.

In 1961, the four surviving members decided to deed 305 acres of the Koreshan property to the state as a historical site. The organization exists today as the World College of Life, a historical organization with headquarters across the highway from the park.

*The Koreshan Settlement at the Koreshan State Park is open from 8 a.m. to 5p.m. every day. Guided tours of the buildings are conducted at 10 a.m. on Saturdays and Sundays from October through May. Estero is twenty-five miles south of Fort Myers on U.S. Highway 41. There is an admission charge for visitors over age six. For further information, call (239) 992-0311.*

# *V*

## *South Florida*

Stranahan House,
Ft. Lauderdale

# South Florida

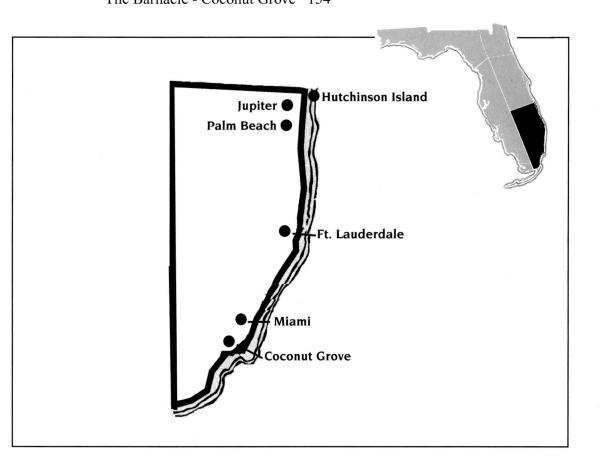

# Tracks to Miami

In the mid-nineteenth century, north Florida and the area around the St. Johns River were rapidly becoming important centers for agriculture and tourism. Key West was flourishing as a capital for salvaging wrecked ships. But the eastern coast and southern tip of the mainland were still largely wilderness.

Its few settlers contended with severe hardships ranging from heat and humidity to hostile Seminoles, who had gradually been pushed further into the swampy Everglades as civilization advanced south. Even remaining in touch with the rest of the world was difficult for those hardy souls living in south Florida. In the 1880s, the sparsely settled area that is now Miami was so remote that it took "barefoot mailmen" three days to hike and row in from Jupiter, ninety miles to the north, with letters and packages. At that time, Dade County stretched all the way north to Jupiter and included part of Lake Okeechobee, near the equally undeveloped Lake Worth area.

By the 1890s, when Henry Flagler pushed his Florida East Coast Railway Co. south of St. Augustine and on into Fort Pierce and Palm Beach, the picture changed dramatically. Flagler had received permission to extend his tracks as far south as present-day Miami in 1892, but he had stopped at Palm Beach in 1894 and built his magnificent resort hotels.

The ambitious Julia Tuttle, who owned 644 acres of woods and marshland north of the Miami River, had tried to persuade Flagler to connect her land with the rest of the east coast. She had no luck until the disastrous freeze of 1894–95, which destroyed the citrus crop even south of Palm Beach. With the withering of the trees, the flow of tourists to fabulous Palm Beach slowed. So when Mrs. Tuttle sent Flagler a branch of fresh orange blossoms from the still-warm south, he pushed on through, arriving in Fort Dallas in 1896.

To the south Florida town—which was then a dozen sand trails that had been cut through dense palmetto, mangroves, and sea grapes—Flagler brought more than a train and the first hotel. As part of his agreement with Mrs. Tuttle and her wealthy neighbors, the William Brickells, he also paved roads, founded an electric company, built a waterworks and sewage system, and helped create the first school, hospital, and newspaper in south Florida. Some citizens wanted to name the new city Flagler, in honor of its benefactor, but he declined.

As civilization rushed to a Miami now linked to Palm Beach, St. Augustine, and points north, its character quickly changed. Incorporated three months after Flagler and his train arrived in 1896, the city was named Miami—perhaps derived from an Indian word for "sweet water" or "big water." It soon became a boom city.

Biscayne Bay and the edge of the Everglades were drained. Residential and tourist developments such as George Merrick's Coral Gables, Glenn Curtiss's Opa-Locka, and, during the Depression, the fabulous home of Florida's art deco hotels, Miami Beach, were quickly begun.

During the boom years, Palm Beach was developing along grander and more lavish, if equally fanciful, lines. The creator of the city's distinctive architecture, Addison Mizner, arrived in Palm Beach in 1918 and set about persuading wealthy visitors to Flagler's hotel that they could have their own mansions for the season. He offered captivating houses in Mediterranean styles—Spanish, Moorish, and Italian, especially Venetian—that looked perfect for the locale.

Mizner's fanciful, flamboyant designs in Palm Beach and, slightly later, in Boca Raton made a permanent imprint on Florida's architecture. For decades, buildings by such noted architects and developers as James Gamble Rogers in Winter Park, George Merrick in Coral Gables, and, just a few years ago, Philip Johnson in Miami were designed in the Spanish style that Mizner made famous.

Bonnet House,
Ft. Lauderdale

# Gilbert's Bar House of Refuge

## Hutchinson Island

This shingled, two-story house—which overlooks the Atlantic Ocean from Hutchinson Island near Stuart—is one of ten structures that once sheltered survivors of shipwrecks along Florida's east coast. Ironically, the house was named for Don Pedro Gilbert, a notorious pirate who operated on the waterways in the area during the early nineteenth century. The shelter opened on March 10, 1876, under the care of keeper Fred Whitehead. He patrolled the beaches for the state during storms and lived in the trim, functional building for a salary of forty dollars a month.

The house's four ground-floor rooms—a bedroom, living room, dining room, and kitchen, with a storage area attached—stand side by side without hallways. The open dormitory for rescued sailors on the second floor is reached by a staircase to one side of the living room. A wide porch encloses the simply arranged rooms, providing protection from sun and rain while allowing breezes to enter the many windows and circulate through the house.

The house sheltered shipwreck survivors for nearly seventy years. Among the more spectacular nearby wrecks was that of the 767-ton *Georges Valentine,* which went aground five hundred yards east of the house in 1904. The ship was carrying $17,000 worth of lumber, which was salvaged and used in a variety of local buildings, and its survivors were sheltered in the house on Gilbert's Bar. At times, the wreck can still be seen from the house, which is the only one of the original ten shelters still standing.

The house served through the Spanish-American War and the First and Second World Wars before being deactivated in 1945. It sat, abandoned, until 1953, when the structure and its 16.8-acre site were purchased by Martin County for $168. The oldest standing structure in the county, the house was restored in 1975 and opened as a historical museum.

Its period furnishings include an old-fashioned kitchen, complete with the restored 1876 fireplace and cast-iron pans, a Victorian settee, and a tilt-top candle stand made between 1780 and 1830. Rows of cots in the upstairs dormitory appear ready to greet survivors, and at the foot of each, a blanket is neatly folded. The keeper's downstairs bedroom features a mahogany spool bed and hand-woven coverlet, both from the early to mid-nineteenth century, and a sampler stitched in 1880 by a ten-year-old girl.

*Gilbert's Bar House of Refuge on Hutchinson Island is open from 10 a.m. to 4 p.m. Monday through Saturday and 1 p.m. to 4 p.m. on Sundays. Admission is charged. For further information, call (772) 225-1875.*

# DuBois House

*Jupiter*

The shingle-style DuBois House overlooking Jupiter Inlet was built by Harry DuBois for his bride in 1898. He had come to Florida from New Jersey in 1887.

DuBois met Susan Sanders, a Jupiter schoolteacher, on a blind date; when he married her, he purchased land to build a home. She had told him that she wanted to be able to see the water from her windows. Their property lay on a twenty-foot-high, ninety-foot-long Jeaga Indian shell mound, and over the years the family sold shell rock from the ancient mound.

The couple's first house was small, and by the time their four children were born, it had become so cramped that DuBois decided to expand it. To the living room, dining room, and bedroom, and kitchen—which, as was typical for Southern frame structures, stood apart from the living quarters—he added three bedrooms and a bathroom in 1903. To do so, he raised the roof and placed a "grandparents'" room and the children's rooms on the new second story.

Lighting in the house was by kerosene lamp. Cypress walls were unpainted, and red-painted floors were covered with handmade rag rugs. The windows had no curtains, for there were no neighbors around. But during the warm months, when mosquitoes and sand fleas were a problem, sheer cotton fabric was tacked over the windows, and every morning they were swept off with a palmetto broom. A palmetto broom was also kept by the door so that those entering the house could brush bugs off their clothes.

Today, although its walls have been painted, the DuBois House is much as it looked in the early years of the century. One change is the coquina rock fireplace, which was built in the 1930s at the request of a couple who rented the house from Susan after Harry's death. The fireplace was constructed of coquina rocks found on the nearby beach.

The house is owned by Palm Beach County and is operated by the Loxahatchee River Historical Society. Many of its furnishings have been donated by family members. The rugs made by Susan and her daughter Anna are on the wooden floors. One

bedroom holds a DuBois commode set, and the old DuBois dining set graces the dining room. The Bahama bed belonged to Harry, and the piano is the one that was used by the DuBois family. In addition, friends of the family donated such period objects as a treadle sewing machine, a kerosene lamp, and a food safe. There is also an oak table from an old house that once stood nearby but has been replaced by condominiums.

*The DuBois House, in DuBois Park in Jupiter on the south side of the Jupiter Inlet, is open for tours Tuesdays and Wednesdays from 1 p.m. to 4 p.m. October through June, and by appointment. No admission is charged. For further information, call (561) 747-8380.*

# Whitehall

## Palm Beach

Henry Flagler built the magnificent Whitehall estate in 1902 as a wedding present for his wife, Mary Lily Kenan. Upon its completion the *New York Herald* proclaimed Whitehall to be "more wonderful than any palace in Europe, grander and more magnificent than any other private dwelling in the world." The home, designed by New York architects Carrère and Hastings, has also been described as "the Taj Mahal of North America." Whitehall's construction cost $2.5 million in 1902, with an additional $1.5 million in furnishings from Pottier and Stymus, a firm based in New York and Paris. Since the Museum was founded in 1959 by Henry Flagler's granddaughter, Jean Flagler Matthews, the Flagler winter home has undergone a vigorous historic preservation campaign.

Whitehall is set on an eight-and-a-half-acre site bordering the Intracoastal Waterway on Palm Beach Island; the 55-room retreat is a testament to the Gilded Age notion that Americans were at the peak of human achievement. Visitors enter through ornate bronze and glass doors with stately lion's head medallions. Once inside they find themselves in the Grand Hall. This marble palace was the largest and grandest of any room in a private American home built during the Gilded Age, complete with an impressive double staircase leading to the second floor. To the visitor, the Grand Hall

might seem smaller than its impressive 4,800 square feet. But, this is exactly what Flagler intended when he asked Carrère and Hastings to drop the ceiling eight feet below what was originally designed in order to give the room a more intimate feel. The Grand Hall's ceiling is decorated with plaster figures and other details. In the ceiling's central dome is a painting depicting "Oracle of Delphi." Two paintings flank the central dome, depicting "Sunrise" to the north and "Sunset" to the south.

Among the other rooms furnished with impressive antiques are the Library; the Music Room, which houses the 1,249-pipe Odell organ; the Grand Ballroom, the Breakfast Room; the French Renaissance–style Dining Room, and the Drawing Room. Most rooms, including the 15 bedrooms located on the second floor, have a particular theme or style, while others feature unique decorative elements, such as the rare aluminum leaf on the walls of the drawing room. In the mid-nineteenth century the process of extracting aluminum was very difficult, making the material more valuable than platinum. The home was built with the latest technology, such as electric lights and indoor plumbing. New building techniques like steel beam construction and plaster ornamentation enabled Whitehall to be built in an incredible 18 months.

The Flaglers entertained the most

prominent members of society and established the tourist season for Florida until Henry Flagler's death in 1913. The home later became a luxury hotel, until Flagler's granddaughter rescued the estate from demolition in 1959. Today, Whitehall is a National Historic Landmark and is open to the public as the Flagler Museum, featuring guided tours, changing exhibits, and special programs. Henry Flagler's private railcar, built in 1886, is on display in the Beaux-arts style Flagler Kenan Pavilion. The Museum is committed to the preservation of Whitehall and educating visitors about American art and life during the Gilded Age.

*The Museum is located at Cocoanut Row and Whitehall Way in Palm Beach. It is open from 10 a.m. to 5 p.m. Tuesday through Saturday, and noon to 5 p.m. on Sunday. Admission is charged; children under age six are free. For more information, call (561) 655-2833 or visit www.flaglermuseum.us.*

# Bonnet House

*Fort Lauderdale*

When Frederic Bartlett built the Bonnet House in Fort Lauderdale between 1920 and 1921, the home was in a quiet, sleepy community. Today, the mansion sits in the middle of a sprawling city, an oasis in a bustling resort.

Set on a thirty-five-acre site with seven hundred feet fronting the Atlantic Ocean, the two-story structure was a winter residence for the amateur architect and his second wife, Helen Birch Bartlett. Bartlett built the thirty-room home of native coral stone, Dade County pine, and concrete blocks that were poured on the site. He imported the second-floor balcony rail from New Orleans, giving the house a Creole look. Later, when bonnet lilies bloomed on the pond near the entrance, Bartlett found a name for his house.

But it wasn't until Frederic married his third wife that the house developed its present whimsical character. Both he and his new wife, Evelyn Fortune Bartlett, were artists. They displayed in their winter residence not only their own work and a variety of collectibles, but also such tropical flora and fauna as orchids, parrots, and monkeys. Secluded behind high concrete walls and iron gates, the Bartletts and their guests could watch black and white swans on the lake in front of the porch.

Inside the elaborate entrance gate that Bartlett designed is the courtyard around which the house was built. A three-tiered fountain plays in its center and is surrounded by palms and other lush tropical plantings. The aviary Frederic built for Evelyn is also in the courtyard, and nearby stands his studio. The studio (the first building on the estate) features a high beamed ceiling, a two-story window that admits the northern light artists so admire, Bartlett's art works and even his original palettes.

In the house, next to the wood-paneled dining room are a simple but well-stocked pantry and kitchen. Mounted fish and sea turtle skulls cover the dining room walls, and china is displayed in three cabinets, along with Frederic's collection of beer steins. In the portico that leads from the dining room to the drawing room is a mural of a Haitian shore-line, with shells pressed into concrete archways and obelisk shapes in the corners. Other features of Bonnet House are its shell museum, a round room in which sets of matched shells found on the beach are shown in cases that line the walls; a bamboo bar where lime cocktails were served; an orchid house and a music room with a fourteen-foot-high ceiling, and a floor painted to look like marble.

In 1983, Evelyn Bartlett willed the then $35 million estate to the Florida Trust for Historic Preservation. It is the most valuable property owned by any state historical society.

*Bonnet House, located at 900 N. Birch Road in Fort Lauderdale, is open Tuesday through Saturday from 10 a.m. to 4 p.m. and Sunday from noon to 4 p.m. Admission is charged. Guided tours are available. Access to the grounds only is available at a reduced admission. Closed Mondays, Thanksgiving, Christmas, New Year's Day, during the Fort Lauderdale Air & Sea Show, and the month of September. For further information, call (954) 563-5393 or visit http://www.bonnethouse.org.*

# King-Cromartie House

*Fort Lauderdale*

This two-story frame house was built in 1907 for Edwin Thomas King. He came to Fort Lauderdale from New Smyrna in 1895, just after the terrible freeze that killed crops all the way to south of Palm Beach in the winter of 1894–95. The next year, King's wife Susan and their four children arrived on the first passenger train to reach Fort Lauderdale.

King, who planted citrus groves and a pineapple field, is best known as a building contractor and boat builder. He constructed many of Fort Lauderdale's buildings, among them the first two schoolhouses, the first courthouse, and the New River Inn. He also brought the first schoolteacher, Ivy Cromartie (later Mrs. Frank Stranahan) to Fort Lauderdale.

The King-Cromartie House is the second one built by King for his family; the first one burned. The 1907 house, which was made of Dade County pine, was originally a one-story structure on the south bank of the New River, opposite and to the west of Frank and Ivy Cromartie Stranahan's trading post and house. The Kings' two-bedroom house had the city's first indoor plumbing and acetylene lighting. Beneath the house was a well from which water was pumped into the house. When electricity became available in 1911, King installed fixtures in each room. That same year, he also built a second floor on the house, adding two bedrooms and a bathroom.

The beams below the house are made of wood salvaged from ships wrecked off the coast. The house is furnished with early twentieth-century pieces, among them Susan King's treadle sewing machine. The house has chairs that could be ordered from the Sears & Roebuck catalog for thirty-seven cents each, and an oak icebox of the sort that was stocked with ice from Miami every day. The piano in the living room was the first in the city, and originally was used in the local Methodist church.

The last family member to occupy the house was Louise King Cromartie, a daughter of Edwin and Susan King. She lived in it with her husband, Bloxham A. Cromartie, the younger brother of Ivy Cromartie Stranahan. In 1971, the Junior League of Fort Lauderdale moved the house to its current location and had it restored. The city now owns it and leases it to the Fort Lauderdale Historical Society.

*The King-Cromartie House is at 231 SW 2nd Avenue in Fort Lauderdale and is part of the Fort Lauderdale Historical Society complex. Group tours are given by appointment. For hours of operation and further information, call (954) 463-4431 or visit www. oldfortlauderdale.org.*

# Stranahan House

## Fort Lauderdale

The gracious two-story frame house on the banks of the New River in Fort Lauderdale was built in 1901 as a trading post/general story and social center. Frank Strahanan's business served the young, rapidly growing community and many Seminoles who lived in the vicinity.

On the first floor was the store, and on the second level was the social center. Meetings, dances, and other festivities were frequently held upstairs which was reached by an exterior stairwell. The wide verandas not only shaded the walls on two floors, they also provided sleeping places for Seminoles who traded at the store.

By 1906, Stranahan's business had become so successful that it had outgrown the building and was moved to a larger structure. Frank and Ivy Cromartie Stranahan—the community's first schoolteacher, whom he had married—renovated the nearly two-thousand-square-foot structure and made it their home.

The Stranahans added an interior stairwell, a chimney and fireplace as the home's only source of heat, and bay windows on the riverfront side. They also installed gas lighting fixtures and partitioned the first floor to conform to its new use as a residence.

By 1913–1915, the Stranahans had made additional changes. The home was wired for electricity and had indoor plumbing. Rooms were also partitioned upstairs. The comfortable frontier home provided the setting to host family and friends—and upon occasion, Henry Flagler.

Change was in the wind, however, when the 1926 and 1928 hurricanes brought the local land boom to an end. Stranahan's business suffered, and in 1929 he took his own life in the nearby New River.

His widow, Ivy, who would become an activist for many causes, continued to live in the house until her death at the age of ninety in 1971. As time passed, additions obscured the house's original outlines. Due to her need to take in paying guests for several years during the winter, small dormers were added for ventilation for her attic living space. The first floor eventually was rented to tenants who used it as a restaurant.

In 1979, the same year the restaurant closed, the house was listed on the National Register of Historic Places. Between 1981 and 1984, the various expansions were removed and the house was restored to its 1913–1915 appearance. It opened to the public in 1984.

*The Stranahan House is on 335 S.E. 6th Avenue (off Las Olas Boulevard at the New River Tunnel) in Fort Lauderdale.. Tour times are 1 p.m. to 4 p.m., with tours on the half-hour, Wednesday through Sunday. The museum is closed the month of September. Admission is charged. For further information, call (954) 524-4736 or visit www.stranahanhouse.org.*

# Vizcaya

## Miami

Vizcaya is one of Florida's grandest homes, an elaborate European-inspired estate that overlooks Biscayne Bay. The gracious villa is approached through a pristine hardwood hammock (native forest) and features ten acres of formal gardens. The gardens are based on French and Italian gardens of the sixteenth to eighteenth centuries, and include fragrant plantings, gazebos, pools, grottoes, mazes, sculptures, cascades, and fountains. Australian pines, popular when Vizcaya was built in the 1910s but now considered an invasive species, have been shaped into fanciful topiary designs.

It took a thousand workers two years to build the $15 million, seventy-room mansion that James Deering named Vizcaya, in honor of a Spanish explorer named Juan Bono de Viscaino. Vizcaya's walls are stone and stucco, and its clay-tiled roof is punctuated by chimneys and sculpted figures from France and northern Italy. On the villa's eastern façade, the high, arched openings of the loggia open onto a terrace that descends by a series of steps to Biscayne Bay. There, in the bay, a stone barge decorated with sculpture by artist A. Stirling Calder serves as a breakwater.

The wonders of Vizcaya don't end at its doors. Inside the thirty-four halls and rooms that are open to the public are countless priceless works of art. Among them are tapestries, Oriental carpets, antique ceilings, and other architectural elements that Deering and his designer Paul Chalfin purchased during several trips to Europe. The pieces range in origin from first-century Rome and fifteenth-century Spain to nineteenth-century France and Italy. They include cedar and bronze doors from the Torlonia Palace in Rome, intricate inlaid-wood chairs from Combe Abbey, England, and sixteenth-century tapestry from Tournai, Belgium, that once belonged to poet Robert Browning.

Signs of opulence are everywhere. In the master bedroom, silk-covered walls rise to a cornice decorated with gilded plaster garlands, and the bed draperies are supported by a French Empire eagle. Silver plaques stud the marble walls of the master bath, in which two sets of 24-karat-gold-plated faucets once controlled

flows of fresh or salt water.

Deering, a bachelor, spent winters at Vizcaya until his death in 1925, and his estate remained in the possession of his heirs until 1952. That year, Deering's heirs generously conveyed the main house and formal gardens to Dade County for a sum below the actual value. They also donated the estate's substantial furnishings and art to the county on the condition that Vizcaya be used as a public museum in perpetuity. It is now Vizcaya Museum and Gardens, a National Historic Landmark and accredited museum.

*The Vizcaya Museum and Gardens, 3252 S. Miami Avenue, Miami, is open from 9:30 a.m. to 4:30 p.m. daily except Christmas. Guided and self-guided tours are available. Admission is charged; there are reduced prices for senior citizens and children. For further information, call (305) 250-9133 or visit www.vizcayamuseum.org.*

# Deering Estate at Cutler

*Miami*

&

In 1913, when Charles Deering bought a twenty-year-old frame structure in Cutler, the village south of present-day Coral Gables at the edge of Biscayne Bay had already seen a brief heyday come and go.

That was fine with Deering, whose father founded the Deering Harvester Machine Company in Maine; a graduate of the United States Naval Academy, he had been a naval attaché in Spain when he built his major art collection, with works by Rembrandt, Goya, El Greco, Velasquez, Degas, Gainsborough, and Murillo, as well as such contemporary Americans as John Singer Sargent and fellow Maine resident Winslow Homer. In 1922, the collection's value was set at $60 million.

Art wasn't Deering's only interest. He had a keen business mind, serving as the first chairman of the International Harvester Co. after its formation in 1902, and was also passionate about botany. Cutler and its pristine environs had a lot to offer. More than forty species of trees live on its 444-acre site, which includes more than 115 acres of coastal tropical hardwood hammocks and 150 acres of pine rockland forests, salt marshes, sand dunes, and mangrove forests. Also appealing were the varieties of birds, marine life and wildlife, from gray foxes to the mangrove cuckoo and black-whiskered vireo, which lived among the gumbo limbo, pigeon plum, and other native plants.

Soon after acquiring his Florida property, Deering began improving it. Cutler was on the land granted to horticulturist Henry Perrine in 1847, at the scene of a skirmish in the Second Seminole War. By 1884, a post office was opened; over the next twenty years, the town grew to comprise thirty pioneer homes, a school, two stores, three docks, and the 1986 two-story vernacular frame house that its original owner had enlarged and turned into an inn in 1900, Richmond Cottage. Deering removed all of the buildings except the Cottage, gradually expanding his estate to include the Carriage House, Power House, and Pump House, between 1916 and 1920.

The most important structure, however, was Stone House, the 14,000-square-foot Mediterranean Revival–style residence that was constructed in 1922, to survive fires and hurricanes and, thus, protect his art collection. Using minimal wood, he required that its solid-concrete walls be eighteen inches thick and that roofs be Cuban barrel tiles, outer doors and windows bronze, with interior sides copper-clad. A water pipeline ran from the main grounds to the surrounding nature preserve, to assure that fires could be extinguished, and his well-stocked wine cellar was hidden throughout Prohibition behind a false bookcase and heavy bank vault–style door.

Deering, whose younger brother built

Vizcaya in nearby Coconut Grove in a more flamboyant style in 1916, seems to have been prescient in his precautions. Until his death in 1927, at age seventy-four, he enjoyed the comforts his winter home, its natural beauty and great archaeological significance. On the Atlantic Coastal Ridge, it counts among its treasures the Tequesta Burial Mound, made between about 1500 and 1700, and fossils from as far back as fifty thousand years, among them mammoth teeth and the bones of dog-size horses, jaguars, sloths, bison, and other ancient species.

When Hurricane Andrew hit south Florida in 1992, Deering's careful attention to solid construction paid off. The estate that had become state property in 1985 and, a year later, an entry on the National Register of Historic Places, was severely damaged. Richmond Cottage lost renovations from 1900 and 1916, so that only the 1896 house remained, but the Stone House stood, structurally intact, with damage only to its more fragile elements: the interior, doors, and windows. But the estate's grounds—especially its tropical hardwood hammocks, rock pinelands, and mangroves—were ravaged.

It took more than six years, but in 1999 Deering Estate reopened; today, visitors can stop at its many attractions and enjoy the man-made and natural beauty that delighted Deering and his guests, and that make his large estate a highlight on Florida's long list of fascinating historic properties.

*The Deering Estate at Cutler is located at 16701 SW 72nd Avenue in Miami. Hours are 9 a.m. to 5 p.m. daily (last admission at 4 p.m.). Admission is $7. For more information, visit www. deeringestate.com or www.co.miami-dade.fl.us/parks/Parks/deer or call (305) 235-1668.*

# The Barnacle

*Coconut Grove*

When Ralph Middleton Munroe first visited south Florida in 1877 at the age of twenty-six, the area was still largely a wilderness. But the Staten Island native's sympathies lay with Ralph Waldo Emerson and the transcendentalist movement's love of nature and adherence to the simple life. So he chose to return south five years later with his wife and her sister. Mrs. Munroe suffered from tuberculosis, and the trip by steamer to Key West and then by small sailboat into Biscayne Bay was difficult. She died while they were camped along the river. Her sister died on the trip back north.

Munroe wintered in Florida for seven years before deciding to move here permanently. He settled in Coconut Grove in 1888 and built his home in keeping with transcendentalist principles, creating his own Walden Pond in Florida. The Barnacle reflects its designer's experience as a ship's builder as well as his beliefs. Its style is simple and direct, in tune with its site and climate. It was originally a one-story Dade County pine structure that stood eight steps above the ground for cross-ventilation and protection from flooding. So that it would survive hurricanes, Munroe anchored The Barnacle to sunken pilings of pitch-pine treated with crude oil as a preservative.

So that he could be an Emersonian "man in the open air," he planned the house as a comfortable, open place that would exist harmoniously with its lush surroundings of tropical plantings. A veranda wrapped around three sides of the house, offering shelter from sun and showers while allowing windows to be kept open. Four corner rooms surround a central, octagonal dining room that features a skylight. When the skylight is open, breezes flow throughout the house.

By 1890, Munroe had remarried and become the father of two children. The house had become cramped. To provide more space, he raised the older structure and added a new ground floor, making The Barnacle a two-story house. Munroe lived in it until his death in 1933. His descendants occupied it until 1973, then sold it to the state so that a portion of Old Florida could be preserved.

The interior of the eleven-room house, finished on the first floor with plaster and on the second with pine paneling, contains many of the late nineteenth-century furnishings Munroe brought with him from his home in New York. Other furnishings include two sixteenth-century European chairs given to Munroe by his across-Biscayne Bay neighbor James Deering, owner of the elegant Vizcaya.

*The Barnacle is located at 3485 Main Highway in Coconut Grove. Tours are scheduled at 10 a.m., 11:30 a.m., 1 p.m., and 2:30 p.m. Friday through Monday (Wednesday and Thursday for groups with reservations). Admission is charged. For further information, call (305) 442-6866 or visit www.floridastateparks.org/thebarnacle.*

# VI
## The Keys

The Little White
House, Key West

# The Keys

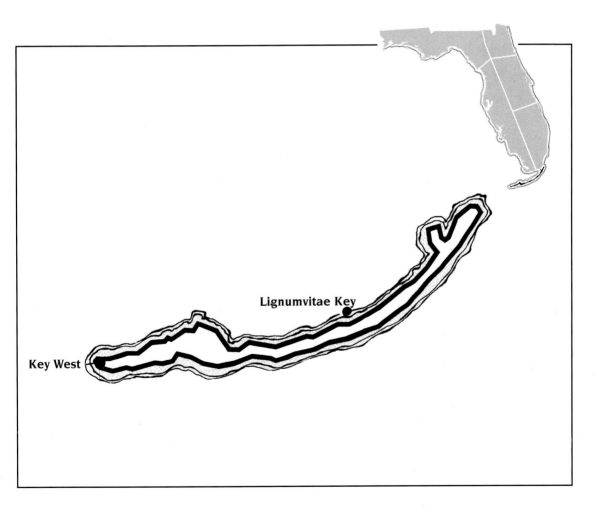

Lignumvitae Key

Key West

# Treasures in the Tropics

Key West and the other small islands that are just south of the peninsula and north of the Florida Straits are not at all typical of the rest of the state. The islands were founded on a seafaring, salvaging economy rather than on agriculture or tourism. They are at a very low elevation—Key West is just four feet above sea level—and their climate and vegetation are more tropical than the rest of Florida.

Just as this region is different, so is its architecture. The architecture that evolved in Key West shows great ingenuity and willingness to synthesize various traditions and indigenous materials.

In 1803, the United States acquired the Louisiana Territory from France, and developed ports along the Gulf coast. These new ports could be reached only through the Florida Straits, one of the busiest shipping routes in the world—and one of the most dangerous. Among the hazards facing captains were the currents, weather, and shallow waters over the coral of the Florida Reef.

Just as worrisome for shippers—and as welcome for the residents of Key West— were the ten thousand or so pirates who sailed between Cuba and Florida. Ships that escaped such legendary outlaws as Blackbeard and Black Caesar often ran out of luck near Key West, where they wrecked on the Reef. Their cargoes were seized by the so-called "wreckers" of Key West, who were able to build and furnish whole houses with their salvaged material. Some of the old houses of Key West were made with salvaged mahogany, which was far less expensive than wood brought south by boat.

Because of the unusual materials available to Key West ships' carpenters, and because of the location and climate, an eclectic style sprang up early. It was called "Conch" after the creators of the style, islanders who ate the meat of the large seashells. These frame structures reflect many influences. Prominent is the airy Bahamian, with open porches, hinged and louvered shutters and encircling verandas on one or two levels. From New Orleans came filigreed trellises and balustrades. Widows' walks on the roofs, usually steeply peaked, show an awareness of New England styles. And many residences have profiles and details that draw from the dominant Greek and Gothic Revivals that swept the nation during Key West's heyday, which ended about the time of the Civil War.

Because of the constant threat of hurricanes, many Key West homes were anchored to the island's underlying coral rock with cypress posts. The wooden building materials may not have been particularly sturdy, but the construction techniques of the Key West houses allowed them to withstand strong winds and waves. Their sills were pegged to the posts that held them in place, and their joints were made without nails, using mortise-and-tenon construction that is beautifully crafted and amazingly durable.

The islanders continued to prosper even after Florida became a territory, in 1821, and federal authorities sought to curb its wrecking activities. Still, in 1855, wrecking brought in millions of dollars in revenue. At that time, the two-by-four-mile city was the most populous in the state, and only the Civil War and the Union blockade of Florida's ports slowed the wrecking-based economy. Near the end of the nineteenth century, it had become a cigar-making center, and many small, wooden structures date from Key West's second period of prosperity.

Those small, functional houses are very different from the eclectic homes of the wreckers, but show an equal facility for adapting to the region. Most are in the so-called "shotgun" style, in which rooms open off a hallway that runs the length of the narrow, rectangular structures. By the end of the century, however, much of the cigar-making industry had shifted to Tampa. In the 1920s, Key West began attracting creative people such as Ernest Hemingway. By the 1960s, it had become a haven for authors like Tennessee Williams and Thomas McGuane.

Old Town Manor,
Key West

# Artist House

## Key West

Built between 1898 and 1900 for artist/ physician Thomas Otto, the Queen Anne– style house features a wealth of colorful stylistic details. An octagonal turret rises above the frame structure's two stories, its seven shuttered casement windows admitting light to a dramatic staircase that curves around the inside of the space. Verandas wrap around the elaborate gabled structure, which is set back from the street in a small garden in typical Key West fashion.

Guests at the splendidly renovated bed-and-breakfast hotel enter through an ornate wrought-iron fence that opens onto five steps up to the pedimented doorway. Everything in the house is impressive, from twelve-foot-high ceilings and tongue-in-groove Dade County–pine floors to the fancy scrollwork that crowns curving columns on the first- and second-story porches.

Thomas Otto was the son of a physician who had been a prisoner of Union soldiers at the dreaded Fort Jefferson in the Dry Tortugas. After the war, Dr. Robert Otto settled in Key West as an apothecary. His son Thomas, one of six children and also a surgeon by profession, built the imposing house on lower Eaton Street and lived in it for forty years.

Among the house's notable features are its blend of styles, its fanciful turret, balconies, jigsaw-cut balustrade, etched-glass transoms, and broad picture windows. The rooms are furnished in a restored Victorian period style, with four-poster high beds, wicker pieces, and William Morris wallpapers.

*Room rates vary at the Artist House, which is located at 534 Eaton Street in Key West. For further information, call (305) 296-3977.*

# Audubon House Museum

*Key West*

When naturalist/artist John James Audubon visited the Florida Keys in 1832, he spent time sketching in the garden of a successful harbor pilot and wrecker, Capt. John Geiger. Geiger's pleasant, Bahamian-style clapboard home had been built for the salvager's large family by ship's carpenters and was filled with furnishings taken from cargoes of ships that had smashed on the treacherous Florida Reef.

The three-story Geiger House now is called the Audubon House Museum. It stands on a now-small lot landscaped with native plantings, but when the famous artist visited in the 1830s, the spacious grounds gave the illustrator of *Birds of America* a great deal of flora and fauna for inspiration. During his stay in the Keys, Audubon sketched nineteen species of water birds that were new to him. Among them were the great white heron and the white-crowned pigeon, which Audubon showed on a branch of a flowering tree from the Geiger garden.

The house is as delightful as the drawings Audubon made during his visit. Its walls are of cypress and southern hardwood that had been brought in from the North. The first- and second-level porches on the front and rear of the shuttered and dormered residence offer shelter from the elements as well as access to cooling breezes.

The home's reconstructed interior is also charming. Among its prized possessions are the collection of Audubon engravings that are on view in a gallery, and fine examples of nineteenth-century furnishings. The curator of the Audubon House collection is implementing a long-range plan to provide insights into home and family life in Key West in the middle decades of the nineteenth century and to recreate a setting that depicts accurately the furnishings of the period.

Occupied by Geiger's heirs for more than 120 years, the house was slated for demolition in 1958. Fortunately, this fine example of early Key West architecture was purchased and restored by the Wolfson Family Foundation. It was among the first such projects in Key West.

*Audubon House Museum, located at 205 Whitehead Street in Key West, is open from 9:30 a.m. to 5 p.m. daily. Admission is charged; children under six are admitted free. Group rates vary. For further information, call (305) 294-2116 or (877) 294-2470.*

# Curry Mansion

## Key West

The ornate Curry Mansion is very different from Key West's typical frame-house design. The house was built in 1899, long after Key West ceased being a wrecker's haven. It is an adaptation of a Paris townhouse that owner Milton Curry, son of the island's first self-made millionaire, saw on his honeymoon. The three-story, eleven-thousand-square-foot Colonial-Revival house's twenty-six rooms include a front parlor, side parlor, dining room, music room, back hall, upper hall, upper rear hall, reception hall, bedrooms for family and servants, and a widow's walk. The broad porch on the clapboard house's façade is topped by a slender, Neo-Classical balustrade that echoes the design of the ground-level railing. In typical Key West style, windows are shaded from sun and rain by hinged Bahama shutters. Windows in seven dormers admit light to the third level, which is reached by a broad staircase and was often used for parties.

Inside, the appointments are just as luxurious and finely detailed. The entrance hall paneling is birdseye maple, and its fretwork, columns, and stair spindles are handmade. The light fixtures in the side parlor are gas and electric. Both were usual in Key West around 1900—and both were unreliable. The buffet, carpet, and glass case in the dining room are part of the house's original, astoundingly posh furnishings. Gold-colored flatware mimics the grandeur of the original Curry service for twenty-four, which was made by Tiffany's and was solid gold.

The 1853 Chickering piano in the music room is said to have come from author Henry James's Newport house, and the lavatory fixtures were imported from China for the house's original owners. Among the wonders in the upstairs rooms are the Tiffany-style beveled glass side and fan windows in the upper hall, the 1868 cherry secretary in a guest bedroom, and, in the attic, a billiard table and racks from approximately 1884. There are six guest rooms in the house, plus fifteen guest rooms with baths around the pool.

*The Curry Mansion, located at 511 Caroline Street in Key West, is open from 10 a.m. to 5 p.m. daily. Admission is charged. For further information, call (305) 294-5349.*

# Old Town Manor

## Key West

The three-story Greek Revival–style Old Town Manor in Key West was built in 1886 by grocer Otis Johnson. Johnson sold the house a few years later to the Curry family, who purchased the house as a wedding present for their daughter Genevieve and her husband, Dr. Warren. A highly respected physician from the University of Pennsylvania, Dr. Warren's home was also his office where he faithfully tended to his patients. In the years the Warrens owned the house, they made several changes and additions. Warren first moved Johnson's grocery, which was next to the house, to the rear of the property, and turned it into a coach house. Genevieve worked hard on the gardens, barging in soil from the Florida Panhandle to grow what would become the island's most prized collection of palm trees. Later, probably during the 1920s or 1930s, as his practice prospered, Warren added a large dining room, enlarged the drawing room, and added two bathrooms. He also added rather formal nineteenth-century-style paneling to the drawing room and dining room walls— and perhaps the beams that run the width of the ten-foot ceilings. The house's floors are polished Dade County pine.

For the most part, Old Town Manor looks as it must have when it was new. The original double doors still welcome you. The entrance of the structure is surmounted by a delicate molded fan design and framed by shutters, as are its pedimented casement windows. The lacy patterns on the railings of the house's two-story porches show a Victorian quality that contrasts pleasantly with such Greek Revival aspects as the slender, squared columns and the emphatic, pedimented façade.

The house became a bed-and-breakfast inn in 1980, when it was purchased by two Englishmen, Sam Maxwell and Denison Tempel. Today's owners, Runi Goyal and Walter Price, both formerly engineers, redecorated with straight lines and bold colors reminiscent of the Victorian era, but with a strong sense of twenty-first-century design. Genevieve's gardens are growing beautifully, and Dr. Warren is still fondly remembered by the community. Some say they still wander their gardens together.

*The Old Town Manor is located at 511 Eaton Street in Key West. Rooms vary seasonally in price. For further information, call (305) 292-2170 or (800) 294-2170.*

# Hemingway Home and Museum
### Key West

When Ernest Hemingway moved into the pleasant two-story, coral-stone house on Whitehead Street in Key West, the house was already eighty years old. The house had been built in 1851 for shipper Asa Tift, and was constructed with stone found on its site. After the coral was quarried, the deep pit that remained became the basement of the Spanish Colonial structure—and at sixteen feet above sea level, the Hemingway House is one of the few in Key West that has a dry cellar.

The house is surrounded by broad verandas on both floors and features tall, arched windows. The writer and his wife Pauline had spent three years in rented quarters in Key West before they bought the old Tift place. After they repaired and renovated the then-decaying house, the couple and their two sons moved in.

Hemingway wrote many of his best-known works here. Among them are *A Farewell to Arms, To Have and Have Not, For Whom the Bell Tolls,* and *The Snows of Kilimanjaro.*

The Hemingways traveled extensively, and on their trips found some of the house's most noteworthy furnishings. The carved eighteenth-century walnut bench in a hall came from a Spanish monastery. The Moorish crystal chandelier overhead is also from Spain. The delicate chandelier over the dining table is of hand-blown Venetian glass, and the room's furnishings are eighteenth-century Spanish. A replica of a ceramic cat given to the author by a friend, Pablo Picasso, sits on a Mexican chest of drawers.

The grounds around the broad-roofed house were planted by Hemingway during the years he lived here, from 1931 to 1939. Hemingway's favorite plants still grow on the acre of land. The pool was a gift from Pauline to her husband. When he learned its price tag—$20,000—he jokingly told her she might as well take his last penny, and pressed the coin into the concrete, where it still may be seen.

Although the marriage ended in 1939 and Hemingway moved to Cuba, Pauline continued to live in the Key West house until the writer's death in 1961. Since 1963, it has been a memorial to Hemingway—and has remained a home to dozens of what are said to be the descendants of his cats.

*The Hemingway Home and Museum, located at 907 Whitehead Street in Key West, is open daily from 9 a.m. to 5 p.m. daily. Admission is charged. For further information, call (305) 294-1136 or visit www.hemingwayhome.com.*

# Little White House

## Key West

Few Americans ever get the chance to visit Camp David, the presidential retreat located just outside Washington, D.C., yet here in south Florida there is a similar site open to the public. It is called the Little White House as it was the winter retreat and functioning White House of the United States from November 1946 through March 1952 during the administration of President Harry S Truman.

The naval station in Key West was established in 1823. During the Civil War, it remained under Federal control and served as the headquarters of the Gulf blockade of the Confederacy. The naval station, however, lacked officers' housing. As early as 1878, officers' complaints were received by Congress. Finally, in January 1890, construction was begun on a two-story Victorian duplex to house the base commandant and base paymaster. The project was completed before Memorial Day on May 30, 1890. Architect George McKay followed government specifications and included six fireplaces and pitched roofs to prevent snow buildup—ironic in a tropical climate. New York contractor Rowland Robbins submitted the low bid of $7,489 to complete the 8,913-square-foot structure. The house was somewhat unique in that it had indoor plumbing and electric lights with electricity provided by a wind charger. It was constructed within feet of the open harbor.

Following nineteen grueling months in office, Truman was exhausted and his health was failing. Admiral Chester Nimitz had just returned to Washington from an inspection tour of the Key West Naval Station and found the Commandant's Quarters unoccupied. The new commander had opted for smaller quarters. Nimitz suggested the warm climate and maximum security would prove an ideal location for the President to rest and relax. Truman came in November 1946 for ten days and set the precedent for later presidents to take working vacations in Key West. During this first visit, Truman went to a captured German submarine and had a dive of 450 feet. This led to speculation as to the real reason Nimitz had suggested the site for Truman's vacation.

The commandant's house was rambling and rustic, with wraparound porches on both floors. Its gray paint was replaced by white in the summer of 1947 and the press immediately began calling it the "Little White House." Following the upset election of 1948, the Navy concluded the building should receive a major remodel as the President would be using it for another four years. Interior designer Haygood Lassiter of Miami was hired with a $35,000 budget to refurnish the house. Likewise, the structure was remodeled at an additional $60,000 to

make the space more usable for Truman's expanding staff and extended stays. In November 1946, Truman had a staff of sixteen plus Secret Service. In March 1952, the staff had grown to fifty-two plus Secret Service and the visit lasted almost a month. Truly, the Little White House had become the functioning White House of America.

In 1947 the Army and Navy were merged at the Little White House into the Department of Defense. Then-General Dwight Eisenhower returned with the Joint Chiefs of Staff in 1948 and 1949 to further this merger. In 1955, now-President Eisenhower had a heart attack and came to Key West to recover. He used the Little White House for meetings during this stay. President John Kennedy in March 1961 had a one-day summit meeting with British Prime Minister Harold Macmillan.

Throughout the Cold War, the Key West Naval Station played a leading role in submarine detection, underwater swimming, and weapons development. Changing technology in March 1974 caused the Key West submarine base to close as nuclear subs were too large for the port. Sadly, the site was abandoned from 1974 through 1986. On January 1, 1987, the house was transferred to the state of Florida for safekeeping. A privately funded restoration was begun and almost a million dollars spent to restore the site to its 1949 appearance.

The site continues to be an important government facility today.

*The Little White House, located at 111 Front Street in Key West, is open for tours 9 a.m. to 4:30 p.m. daily. Admission is charged; children under 5 are admitted free. Tours are available every 15 minutes and last approximately one hour. For more information call (305) 294-9911 or visit www.trumanlittlewhitehouse.com.*

# Louie's Backyard

*Key West*

The two-story frame house that is now Louie's Backyard restaurant was built around 1900 for Capt. James Randall Adams. He was a wrecker who made a fortune salvaging goods from ships destroyed off Key West. During his lifetime, it is said, Adams boasted that everything that went into the home, including its front and side verandas on both levels and its Doric columns, was merchandise that had been salvaged.

Adams's gracious, Dade County–pine house was built in the Classical Revival style with a tin roof, ten rooms, and ceilings twelve feet high. Its kitchen—like others in Key West and in Florida in general—was in a building separate from the rest of the house so that heat and the danger of fire would be kept as far as possible from the living quarters. A narrow porch on the back, along with the porches on the front and sides, allowed cooling breezes to enter windows left open during showers and shaded the walls from the sun.

The residence stayed in the Adams family for a number of years. It then changed hands several times before 1971, when it was purchased by Frances and Louis Signorelli, who opened the patio, living room, and dining room into a small restaurant known as Louie's Backyard. That Louie's seated about twenty, had one waiter, and operated out of a cigar box cash register.

In 1983, Phil and Pat Tenney and Proal Perry bought the house from the Signorellis. They renovated the house and doubled the dining space. They also opened the upstairs for private parties.

Today's Louie's Backyard includes a large dining room addition, enlarged terrace, and high, modern windows on its first and second floors as well as the Afterdeck Bar at the water's edge. The renovated house is listed on the National Register of Historic Places.

*Louie's Backyard is located at 700 Waddell Avenue in Key West. Lunch is from 11:30 a.m. to 3 p.m., dinner from 6 p.m. to 10:30 p.m. For further information, call (305) 294-1061.*

# Wrecker's Museum

## Key West

❧

This simple frame house, which now is the Wrecker's Museum in Key West, probably was built around 1829 and is the oldest in the city. One of its earliest owners—and perhaps its builder—was a jack-of-all-trades named Richard Cussons. He had come north from Nassau in the Bahamas around 1828 and may never actually have lived in the house.

In Key West, Cussons became a carpenter, grocer, and auctioneer. During his early years in the city, his two-story, Dade County–pine structure was probably at the corner of Whitehead and Caroline Streets. At some point, it was moved to its present site on Duval Street, where it presumably was added to another house.

It became the home of a merchant seaman and wrecker, Capt. Francis B. Watlington, around 1829. Born in the Virgin Islands, Watlington had come to Key West from New York with his sixteen-year-old bride around 1828, and moved into the then-new "Oldest House" soon afterward. Watlington replaced the clapboard house's roof scuttles—or ship's hatches—with three dormer windows, which were graduated in size. All of the house's windows were shuttered to protect them from stormy weather.

Like other residences of its period and later, the Wrecker's Museum shows a variety of influences, not the least of which is that of a ship's carpenter. There is a ship's hatch on the roof and a "landlubber's tilt"—a crooked wall and window—in the captain's office. The building is raised three feet from the ground on lime-rock piers for air circulation. Its kitchen, which stands about twelve feet from the house to keep the heat generated there from the rest of the main wooden structure, has an open fireplace and a wall oven. This outside kitchen is the only original one still standing in the Keys.

The simple cottage-type house was planned around a long hall that opens into two front parlors, with a dining room on one side and a bedroom (now used as a caretaker's quarters) on the other. Off the porch is the captain's office, opposite another bedroom that is closed to the public. Most of the Oldest House's nine rooms are decorated with nineteenth-century furnishings and a variety of objects from Key West history, and many of the objects are original to the house. Among them are antique toys including an 1850s Conch-style dollhouse scaled one inch to one foot.

*The Oldest House (now the Wrecker's Museum), 322 Duval Street in Key West, is open from 10 a.m. to 4 p.m. daily. Admission is charged. For further information, call (305) 294-9502.*

# Matheson House

*Lignumvitae Key*

The Matheson House and the wilderness surrounding it transport visitors to a much earlier, simpler time. A windmill that once provided power for the residence still stands on the property, and a twelve-thousand-gallon cistern still holds fresh water channeled from the roof.

The Matheson House was built in 1919 on Lignumvitae Key for the caretaker of William J. Matheson. Matheson was a wealthy chemist who owned Lignumvitae Key and resided on another of his south Florida islands, Key Biscayne near Miami.

The Matheson House was made of Key Largo limestone, a fossil coral rock that is found on many of the upper Florida Keys. Most of the stones used on the Matheson House were collected when the five-acre site was cleared for construction. The Dade County pine used on the building's interior is a dense, durable wood that was then readily available. The resinous pine resists insects and weather damage, making it ideal for the location.

The house has four bedrooms, indoor plumbing, a wood-burning stove, and an icebox. The house is raised about ten feet off the ground, putting it well above sea level. Besides protecting the house from possible flooding, the elevation permits air to circulate below, keeping the house cool and keeping away mosquitoes. After it was damaged in the Labor Day hurricane of 1935, the house's original flat, red-tiled roof was replaced by a pitched roof shingled with cedar.

The house is furnished as it was in the late 1930s, when Capt. Abner Sweeting and his family lived in it. While he was the island's caretaker, Sweeting made three miles of graded trails, placed six cannons salvaged from a wreck on Carysfort Reef in the front yard as decorations, and raised a variety of animals. Among them were Mexican burros, round-ear rabbits, sacred geese, and Galapagos tortoises.

The house itself is not the only

attraction. Around it lies a virgin tropical forest of the kind that existed on most of Florida's upper Keys before advancing civilization scraped the thin layer of vegetation off the coral-reef islands. The exotic plants around Matheson House include mastic, strangler fig, gumbo limbo, pigeon plum, and poisonwood.

*Three-hour boat tours to the house leave from Indian Key Fill on U.S. 1 at 1:30 p.m. Thursday through Monday. Admission is charged. Visitors should have walking shoes and mosquito repellent. For reservations, call (305) 664-4815.*

# Other Houses

## Jamie's French Restaurant
### Pensacola

Pensacola's tiny, gingerbread-trimmed Jamie's French Restaurant is characteristic of the Victorian-style dwelling known as the Gulf Coast Cottage. It was built in the early 1860s of native yellow pine and local brick, with large windows and high-ceilinged rooms opening off a center hall.

The cream-and-apricot cottage, constructed by attorney J. B. Jones a block from Pensacola Bay, stands on the site of an earlier Spanish settlement. As was often the practice on the Gulf coast at the time, the floor plan of the house was long and narrow to fit on long narrow lots. Rooms were arranged one behind the other, railroad-car style, on either side of the hallway. The two bedrooms were opposite the parlor and dining room, and the kitchen was across the back. The structure's hip roof extends over the broad porch, whose brackets and

railing are decorated with cutwork trim. The house retains its original two chimneys and four fireplaces, which are still the only means of heating the house, although the two bedrooms now serve as a large dining room with an open fireplace. Floors are of yellow pine planks and ceilings are of pine beadboard.

*Jamie's French Restaurant, 424 Zaragoza Street in Pensacola, specializes in classic French cuisine. Lunch is served Tuesday through Saturday from 11:30 a.m. to 2:30 p.m. Dinner is served Monday through Saturday from 6 p.m. to 10 p.m. For further information, call (850) 434-2911.*

## Brokaw-McDougall House
### Tallahassee

When Peres Bonney Brokaw arrived in Tallahassee in 1840, he was young and unmarried. He had moved from New Jersey to Alabama and then, in the late 1830s, to Florida, where he went into the livery business and prospered. In 1850, he married. Six years later, as his family grew, he began constructing the Italianate, two-story mansion that would stand as one of the few of its type.

By 1860, the clapboard house—which had overhanging eaves and a broad front porch supported by six Corinthian columns—was complete, as was the landscaping on Brokaw's property. The house remained in the family until 1973, when the descendants of the original owners sold it to the state of Florida.

The eight-room house, which is managed by the City of Tallahassee Parks and Recreation Department, has been completely restored to the style of the mid- to late nineteenth century. The gardens were restored in 1976 as a bicentennial project of the Florida Federation of Garden Clubs and the Tallahassee Preservation Board.

Shutters hang on large casement windows on the house, which has been repainted in its 1884 colors—Tuscan yellow with green and brown trim. A graceful balustrade surrounds the veranda on the second story. Each of the symmetrically arranged rooms, which open off a long hall, has a high ceiling. The square plan culminates in a square cupola at the center of the peaked, shingled roof. Trim brackets project from the wide eaves, punctuating the house's proportions and adding a decorative element.

Interior features include large halls running the length of both floors. The rooms on either side of both upstairs and downstairs hallways are identical in size. On the second floor, they are separated by bathrooms that were originally used for storing trunks. Several rooms are furnished in the style of the period when the house was new.

*The Brokaw-McDougall House, located at 329 North Meridian in Tallahassee, is open Monday through Friday from 9 a.m. to 5 p.m. There is no admission charge. For further information, call (850) 891-3900.*

## I. W. Phillips House
*Orlando*

One of three historic houses that form a bed-and-breakfast complex in downtown Orlando, the I. W. Phillips House was built in 1916 right next door to the current location of the Norment-Parry Inn. The gracious two-story residence was constructed not of the ubiquitous pine that was so favored before the turn of the nineteenth century in Florida, but of the sturdier oak.

In typical vernacular style, the I. W. Phillips house had tall, large windows so that its interior could be cooled by breezes from nearby Lake Lucerne in what is now Orlando's main historic district, east of Orange Avenue and just south of the business section. This particular home was stately from the start, with its high ceilings and spectacular central staircase.

The I. W. Phillips House, like the two

other historic homes on its brick-paved, landscaped central courtyard, has been styled to suggest the comfortable lifestyle of wealthy central Floridians in the early years of this century. The house itself was moved to its current site in 1946, when then-owner Wellborn Phillips built a new apartment block. During its 1988 renovation, the house gained the two-story veranda that wraps around three sides.

Its window-filled walls were opened up even more, with French doors that open onto the front and side porches, and the dark wood floors throughout were given a new luster and richly patterned Oriental area rugs. Its furnishings are elegant Edwardian, heavy and somber, and its art works range from an immense breakfront in which fine pieces of Oriental porcelain are displayed to massive, ornate furnishings, some rescued from a grand Old Florida hotel, and impressive academic oil paintings.

The staircase rises to a landing dominated by a magnificent floral stained-glass window from the studios of nineteenth-century design genius Louis Comfort Tiffany. The wide front porch with overhead paddle fans, metal lawn chairs and tables, and lush landscaping, overlooks a terrazzo dance floor and fountain. The decor is enormously evocative of its era. More than most, this Orlando historic home feels like a home, despite its popularity as a reception hall–cum–urban inn.

*The I. W. Phillips House, 211 N. Lucerne Circle East in Orlando, is open throughout the year for parties, as a hotel, and for visitors. For more information, call (407) 648-5188.*

## Norment-Parry Inn
### Orlando

The downtown Orlando Norment-Parry Inn was built for Judge Richard B. Norment of Baltimore and his wife, Margaret Parry, between 1883 and 1885, as their permanent home. It was built at a time when Orlando was a small community with sandy roads and a largely agrarian economy. The oldest documented house extant in Orlando, this two-story Victorian structure is now a bed-and-breakfast hotel.

A wide, open porch projects from its

frame façade, and the screened porch on the east side on the ground floor, like the tall, narrow windows throughout, offers light and cross-ventilation. Among its original features are the ornate, typically Victorian wooden scrollwork on the front-porch columns and interior woodwork.

The house was built of Florida hardwood. The L-shaped structure was enlarged in the 1920s, when gas lighting was installed. In 1986, it was renovated and refurbished in a fanciful Victorian style to become a bed-and-breakfast inn. Its seven guest suites, parlor, and other rooms are furnished with American and English antiques.

*The Norment-Parry Inn is located at 211 N. Lucerne Circle E. in Orlando. Room rates vary. For further information, call (407) 648-5188.*

## Wellborn Apartments
*Orlando*

Like its adjacent historic homes at The Courtyard at Lake Lucerne, the I. W. Phillips House and the Norment-Parry Inn, the Wellborn Apartments were built on the shores of Lake Lucerne in downtown Orlando's residential district. And like its neighbors at The Courtyard, it was a structure that had fallen into some disrepair with the passage of time and was restored during the 1980s. The difference between them is that while the other two were single-family homes, the Wellborn was originally designed for multifamily life.

The solid block structure that rose on its

lakefront site in 1946—just at the outside edge of "historic" for our purposes—is in a restrained art deco/art moderne mode, with an intriguing and rather late variant of the more severe "form-follows-function" International style of the 1920s and 1930s. Its series of cubes, joined at the sides, have been angled to take full advantage of its lake views.

It attracted the elite of Orlando, then a small and leisurely Southern town, and was the site of many social functions—particularly the memorable late-afternoon cocktail parties that were held on its rooftop sundeck. Room decor ranges from the exotic Thai room, an outré addition to the art deco aesthetic, to the "high-deco" of Room 311, whose lighting fixtures were salvaged from a period building undergoing renovation, and the "fabulous fifties" room with kidney-shaped tables and a zebra-covered sofa.

The Wellborn owners have been commended by the city of Orlando's Historic Preservation Department for retaining or reconstructing all its original features, including metal casement windows—charming in corners—decorative door screens, porthole windows, classic ironwork, and lighted sign. Shady and welcoming, the pink-painted art deco Wellborn brings to life an older, more colorful Florida.

*The Wellborn Apartments at The Courtyard at Lake Lucerne, 211 N. Lucerne Circle East in Orlando, just south of the downtown business district, are open throughout the year. For more details, call (407) 648-5188.*

## St. Clair Whitman House
*Cedar Key*

While the small Cracker house at the center of the Cedar Key Museum State Park offers a charming view of life in coastal 1920s Florida, what sets it apart is what it shows about its late owner's interest in nature and natural history.

St. Clair Whitman was named for the town where he was born in 1898, St. Clair, Missouri. In 1921, he bought and expanded the Cracker cottage Henry Hale had built in 1880 on Goose Cove and lived there with his family. It sat empty for years after he died in 1959, and was set for demolition when his descendants offered it to anyone who would save it—an offer taken up by local citizens and politicians and the state of Florida.

It was moved to its current location in the state park in 1991 and restored to its 1920s appearance. The cottage has a wide front porch, metal roof, cedar-shake exterior walls, heart pine flooring and beaded wainscoting, and some cypress elements. Its style is a simple "hall and parlor," with the hall leading from the front door to the rear rooms; curtains separate the wide hall from the dining room and kitchen. The original iron bed still stands in the bedroom, near quilts and a treadle sewing machine. In the kitchen, a kerosene stove made in Cleveland strikes a lively pastel note—its turquoise enamel is far brighter than the upright piano in the parlor. The icebox and cypress table in the kitchen are displayed with period crockery, milk bottles, and a china cabinet. Each room was lit by two oil lamps until electricity was installed in 1927.

Probably the most unique aspect of the house, however, is the space Whitman dedicated to his collections. Today, the house is surrounded by the sort of flora and fauna that fascinated him: native sand pine, slash pine, red cedar, live oak, sabal palm, saw palmetto, yaupon, and coonties, as well as the butterflies and birds they attract, and the seashells, vintage photographs, native Timucuan artifacts, and other objects that he collected.

Whitman carefully catalogued each item and installed the collections in his own museum, many in cigar boxes, and in 1955 *National Geographic* magazine showcased it. When he died four years later, Whitman donated his collections to the people of Cedar Key; most are now in his house museum, with some works on display at the local Historical Society Museum.

*The St. Clair Whitman House, located at Cedar Key Museum State Park, 12231 SW 166 Court in Cedar Key, is open 9 a.m. to 5 p.m. Thursday through Monday. For fees and details visit http://www.floridastateparks.org/cedarkeymuseum or call (352) 543-5567.*

## Bronson-Mulholland House

*Palatka*

When Judge Isaac Bronson built Sunny Point for his wife Sophronia and their two daughters, Gertrude and Emma, in 1854, it was a grand three-story frame home that stood in the heart of bustling young Palatka in a Florida just emerging from the Seminole Wars.

Today, after extensive restorations during the 1970s and a listing on the National Register of Historic Places in 1973, it is still among the grandest and oldest of Florida's antebellum mansions, and a fine example of Florida vernacular architecture.

What makes it even more remarkable is how Sunny Point, which is now known as the Bronson-Mulholland House, spent the past century and a half. Bronson was a judge in New York from 1822 until 1840, except for two years in the U.S. Congress. He then came down to Florida to serve as a federal and then circuit judge.

When the judge and his family moved to Palatka, on the St. Johns River, it was a boomtown as the St. Johns' paddle steamers brought in tourists escaping cold northern winters. The Bronsons built a solid house, with echoes of the Greek Revival style that flourished at the time, but that also was adapted to the hot, humid weather of their new climate. Porches wrap around the first and second stories, offering shelter from the sun and from rain that might otherwise dampen the interior when the tall casement windows that stood in symmetrical arrangement along clapboard walls were open to admit cooling breezes.

The house is raised on brick piers and crowned today with the red metal roof that replaced the original shingles. Dormers rise from the roof, as do chimneys, and broad steps lead up to a front door that includes a glazed transom and sidelights under a high, gracious pediment. Other neo-classical elements are the paneled framing under each of the ground-floor windows, and the linear tracery of the wraparound veranda's upstairs railings.

The judge died in 1855 and during the Civil War the house was occupied first by Confederate troops, then by Union soldiers. In 1866, it became a school for freed slave children. After that it had a checked history and was finally converted to apartments. In 1965, the city of Palatka bought the property and, although it had deteriorated so much that it was slated for demolition, gave the Putnam County Historic Society its use. The Society began restorations and won Sunny Point its historic designation as the Bronson-Mulholland House.

*The Bronson-Mulholland House, located at 100 Madison Street in Palatka, is open 2 p.m. to 5 p.m. Monday through Thursday and Sunday. For information, visit www.rootsweb.com/~flpchs/bmhren or call (386) 329-0140.*

## Coral Gables House

*Coral Gables*

This plantation house was the boyhood home of George Merrick, founder of the city of Coral Gables. The house was built about 1906 of a local fossil-bearing limestone that, according to legend, the Merricks mistook for coral.

The two-story, six-bedroom Coral Gables House replaced the earlier frame structure that the young George and his Congregational minister father, the Rev. Solomon Merrick, had constructed when they first arrived in south Florida from Massachusetts in 1899 to grow fruit and vegetables. Mrs. Merrick and her four younger children arrived in Florida later. The family had spent their life savings of $1,100 to buy the land. Together, the Rev. Merrick and his son converted their 160-acre pine-wood wilderness into a garden. After cultivating it, the Merricks became the largest exporters of grapefruit in the Southeast.

Designed by George's mother Althea, Coral Gables House shows a fine adaptation of a sedate, Classical New England style to a new climate and a new set of building materials. A graceful Palladian window is set into a triangular area over the roof of the broad, ground-level porch, and a small pediment over the columned entryway repeats the shape of the roofline. The building materials Mrs. Merrick chose for her home were practical and readily available: oolitic limestone and durable Dade County

pine for the house itself, and concrete for the columns that support the porch. The house was raised above the ground to allow cross-ventilation and to protect it from flooding. Its steeply pitched, gabled roof featured a coral-colored tile.

Coral Gables House has been restored and is decorated with period furnishings from the 1920s, many of which belonged to the Merrick family.

*The Coral Gables House, 907 Coral Way in Coral Gables, is open from 1 p.m. to 4 p.m. Wednesday and Sunday. Admission is charged. For further information, call (305) 460-5361.*

# Index

## Photo Credits

**Line drawings** by H. Patrick Reed & Nan E. Wilson

**25** West Florida Historic Preservation Inc. **27** West Florida Historic Preservation Inc. **29 top** West Florida Historic Preservation Inc. **29 bottom** Dean DeBolt. **31** Florida Department of Environmental Protection. **33** Florida State Parks. **35** Florida State Parks. **37** Florida State Parks. **39** Courtesy of Tall Timbers Research Station & Land Conservancy. **41** Tallahassee Trust for Historic Preservation, Inc. **43** Amanda Chamberlain Hammerli. **45** Courtesy of the Knott House Museum. **47** Courtesy of the Tallahassee Museum. **49** Lauren Raulerson. **55** National Park Service. **57** Courtesy of the Casa de Solana. **59** Courtesy of the St. Augustine Historical Society. **61** RGT Photos. **63** Courtesy of the Raintree Restaurant. **65** Courtesy of the St. Augustine Historical Society. **67** Courtesy of the Victorian House Bed & Breakfast. **69** Courtesy of the Bayfront Westcott House. **71** Erik Kvalsvik. **77** Dudley Farm Historic State Park. **79** Karen Kirkman, Historic Haile Homestead Inc. **81** Courtesy of the Alachua County Historic Trust: Matheson Museum, Inc. **83** Courtesy of Herlong Mansion Historic Inn & Gardens. **85** Florida State Parks. **87** Courtesy of The Casements. **89** Volusia County Government. **91** Courtesy of the Bradlee-McIntyre Museum. **93** Courtesy of The Captain and The Cowboy. **95** Harry P. Leu Gardens. **97** City of Cocoa. **99** Courtesy of the Museum of Arts & Sciences, Inc. **101** Courtesy of the Maitland Historical Society. **103** Courtesy of the Thurston House B&B. **105** Courtesy of the West Volusia Historical Society, DeLand House Museum. **107** Courtesy of the Mary McLeod Bethune Foundation, Bethune-Cookman University. **109** Courtesy of the Seven Sisters Inn. **111** Courtesy of the Eustis Historical Museum & Preservation Society, Inc. **117** Courtesy of the Ybor City Museum State Park. **119** Courtesy of the Banyan House Bed & Breakfast. **121** Florida State Parks. **123** Courtesy of the John and Mable Ringling Museum of Art. **125** Guptill House at Historic Spanish Point, staff photo (Laura Dean). **127** Robin Harvey, R Studio, Matlacha. **129** Courtesy of the Edison & Ford Winter Estates. **131** Courtesy of the Edison & Ford Winter Estates. **133** Florida State Parks. **139** Linda Geary. **141** Kathleen Glover, Jupiter, Florida. **143** Courtesy of the Henry Morrison Flagler Museum, Palm Beach, Florida. **145** Courtesy of the Bonnet House Museum & Gardens. **147** Courtesy of the Fort Lauderdale Historical Society. **149** Courtesy of Stranahan House, Inc. **151** Bill Sumner for Vizcaya Museum and Gardens. **153** Courtesy of Brian Call. **155** Florida State Parks. **161** Alex Caemmerer. **163** The Audubon House & Tropical Garden. **165** Courtesy of the Curry Mansion Inn. **167** Courtesy of Old Town Manor. **169** Courtesy of the Hemingway Home and Museum. **171** Courtesy of the Truman Little White House. **173** Courtesy of Louie's Backyard. **175** Courtesy of the Oldest House Museum and Gardens. **177** Florida State Parks. **Front cover** Florida State Parks. **Back cover, left to right** Courtesy of the John and Mable Ringling Museum of Art; Courtesy of the Seven Sisters Inn; Courtesy of the Victorian House Bed & Breakfast.